RICHARD BURTON

Her eyes blazed with violet and violent electricity, but before she could spark again, Richard wagged his finger. 'We'll have no more of that . . . You'll be giving a bad impression. Of course, there's publicity. It's necessary and I don't blame anyone for doing his job . . . Who didn't read all about Liz and myself?'

And then, quite casually, he looked straight into Elizabeth's eyes and said: 'I want to marry Elizabeth, and I will marry her. There have been all kinds of rumours, but that is what is going to happen. No ifs. No buts. She wants to marry me. I want to marry her.'

So at last it was confirmed – firmly, officially, exclusively. I broke the news . . .

Fergus Cashin is a well-known Fleet Street columnist and showbusiness writer. His film and theatre criticisms are syndicated throughout the world. He has also ghosted a number of show-business autobiographies.

D1353650

RICHARD BURTON

Fergus Cashin

A STAR BOOK

published by
the Paperback Division of
W. H. ALLEN & Co. Ltd

A Star Book
Published in 1984
By the Paperback Division of
W.H. Allen & Co. Ltd
A Howard & Wyndham Company
44 Hill Street, London W1X 8LB

First published in Great Britain by W.H. Allen & Co. Ltd, 1982

Printed in Great Britain by
Hunt Barnard Printing Ltd, Aylesbury, Bucks.

ISBN 0 352 31311 0

Acknowledgements

THE AUTHOR WOULD like to thank the Jenkins' family —
brothers and sisters of the subject of this biography — and the
many school friends and actors, actresses, producers and
directors who were generous enough to give time to memory
and to help shape the various stages in the life of Richard
Burton.

In particular he acknowledges the valuable work and shared
experiences of his good friend and long time colleague John
Cottrell.

He is grateful also to *Time* magazine for the extract which
appears on pages 28–29; and to *The Observer* for permission
to reproduce the theatre review of the late Mr Kenneth Tynan
on pages 103–104.

Chapter One

JUST HOW ĐIFFICULT it is to write biography can be reckoned by anybody who sits down and considers just how many people know the real truth about his or her love affairs. Sex is, as Rebecca West implies, the real stuffing of biography; and I much admire those who, never having met the subject of their research, let alone their paramours, feel compelled to commit to paper today what was in the newspapers yesterday.

Two recent biographies of that ilk have detailed the lives of Richard Burton and Elizabeth Taylor without ever once coming anywhere near the true flesh — that real truth which Burton's Welsh schoolmaster of elementary days described as 'a shadowy, untouchable threequarter forever jinking down a ghostly touchline'. Those who tackle the public shadow rather than private substance are those who, as one of the biographers so aptly put it, 'find themselves so overcome by fame that it inspires a kind of lunacy on the part of the unfamous'. It could be, of course, that the unfamous (journalists like myself) inspire a sort of lunacy on the part of the famous.

Indeed this is what happened some twenty years ago when Burton and Taylor appeared in *Cleopatra* and rubbed bodies together more vigorously off stage than they did on set. It wasn't an unusual occurrence in the movie business and would have passed unnoticed had not Elizabeth surprised the industry, and her husband Eddie Fisher in particular, by the slavery of her passion for Burton who found himself hoist by his own promiscuous petard. In the male dominated and well protected permissiveness of the dream factory she delighted in Burton's outrageous cockadoodling and his cheerful indifference to consequence. But what he failed to see in his daring courtship and her public submission was a reversal of the roles. The prey had become the huntress: the hunter the prey. He believed in monogamy and his understanding wife Sybil. So did Elizabeth, but she had always pursued monogamy from bed to bed.

Her story was well known, but strangely enough in those seemingly forgotten days when gay was gaiety, the pill was Beechams and the morals of Mrs Whitehouse were the majority opinion, the public were romantically sympathetic to movie queens they had known since they were celluloid princesses. A wartime generation of housewives caught up in the awful wedded anxiety of aloneness or the boredom of togetherness had known Elizabeth since she rode to victory in the Grand National as twelve-year-old Velvet Brown. She was their escape from reality. Her search for happiness was their felicity.

They were thrilled when she married Conrad Nicholson Hilton as an eighteen-year-old virgin and made her first pronouncement on monogamy. 'Your heart knows when you meet the right man. There is no doubt that Nicky is the one I want to spend my life with.' Life with Nicky lasted a brief eight months. In less than a year she was pursuing a reluctant Michael Wilding who was actually in love with Marlene Dietrich and wedded to Kay Young when Elizabeth made *his* mind up by buying her own engagement ring and securing him an offer he couldn't refuse — a three year MGM contract at $3,000 a week. When she married him in Caxton Hall, she said, 'I just want to be with Michael, to be his wife. He is twice my age and so mature and that is what I need.' But two babies later she was in the arms of another — Mike Todd, more than twice her age, already engaged to Evelyn Keyes and the ex-husband of Joan Blondel.

She announced the betrothal while still married to Wilding by saying, ' I love Mike Todd. I love him passionately, absolutely passionately.' With a baby on the way she married the producer of *Around the World in 80 Days* on 7 February, 1957. Eddie Fisher serenaded the couple during the ceremony by singing a Mexican wedding song. Fourteen months later Mike was killed in an air crash and his wedding day songster was publicly romancing Elizabeth with 'Another bride, another groom, another sunny afternoon'.

Elizabeth converted to the Jewish faith and married Eddie in a synagogue on the day his wife Debbie Reynolds divorced him saying, 'We will be on our honeymoon for thirty or forty years.'

The honeymoon lasted barely thirty months, yet in that time Elizabeth, unlike Ingrid Bergman whose career was seriously damaged by her adulterous affair with Italian director Roberto Rossellini, not only managed to ride out the storm of public indignation but shone back as a bigger star than ever by winning an Oscar for *Butterfield 8* after being nominated and snubbed by the Academy for a much better performance in *Cat on a Hot Tin Roof*. The feeling among her peers was expressed by the Theatre Owners of America who named her as 'Star of the Year' for *Cat* and then withdrew the award because 'the movie industry is at the mercy of public opinion and to award Miss Taylor the honour at a time like this is simply out of the question'. Elsa Maxwell described her as 'aggressive in her romances, ruthless in her disregard for the feelings of those who have stood for marriage, and indifferent to the wreckage she has left behind her'. The period of transition, from the callous marriage-wrecker to the resurrection of a woman wronged, happened during the filming of the first version of *Cleopatra* in London and had nothing to do with the revelation that Debbie Reynolds's matrimonial bed had been a chaste couch long before the arrival of Elizabeth.

She had demanded and got a million dollars for sixty-four days' work on *Cleopatra* plus $3,000 a week for living expenses, two penthouse suites at the Dorchester and a Rolls to take her to the studios. It was the biggest deal ever swung by a movie actress, and when producer Walter Wanger told Spyros Skouras, president of 20th Century-Fox, that Elizabeth was ready to sign, the Greek tycoon hesitated.

He wanted to play safe with his contract star Joan Collins. His hesitation cost the financially troubled studio dearly. Instead of coming down in price when Wagner told her the rest of the Fox executives were on his side Elizabeth, who desperately wanted the part, upped the ante. She now wanted the studio to abandon Cinemascope and use her late husband's Todd A-O. On top of these royalties she demanded ten per cent of the gross. Skouras threw in his hand.

On the very first day of shooting in September 1960 Rouben Mamoulian received confirmation of Skouras's fears with the news that Elizabeth was ill. The *Daily Mail* reported later in the month that she was hiding in her hotel because she was too fat to appear on set. It turned out to be toothache.

In October she was burning with Malta fever and, after another spell in the London Clinic, she was ordered to take a long rest. Chaos reigned at Pinewood Studios. There were hold-ups through a Hairdressers' Union strike and troubles with script, costumes and weather. 'It was sheer lunacy,' said Mamoulian. 'The insurance people were full of nervous chicken. They said "Shoot some film, shoot anything — as long as you can keep the film going." Well, we tried. Rain, mud, slush and fog. It was stinking weather. We didn't have one inch of film with Liz in it.' By mid-January Elizabeth was ready for work. But now there were new problems. Mamoulian had resigned; Caesar (Peter Finch) and Antony (Stephen Boyd) were committed elsewhere; the script was judged unsatisfactory and the twelve minutes of useless celluloid in the can was dumped. The film was shelved and Elizabeth went back to bed and celebrated her twenty-ninth birthday with influenza. It didn't rate a paragraph in Fleet Street. Joseph Mankiewicz replaced Mamoulian at a cost of three million dollars and was given two months to save the picture. Elizabeth's illnesses were becoming a joke — a sick joke as far as the shareholders of Fox were concerned.

But a week later the girl who was always crying wolf had the Fox men in tears of anxiety. On 4 March, eleven doctors including Lord Evans, the Queen's physician, were at her bedside and newspapers put their reporters on a round the clock watch outside the London Clinic. Her breathing had almost stopped. 'The prognosis is not good,' her press agent told reporters. 'She is suffering from staphylococcus

11

pneumonia and is in a critical condition.'

The night before a young doctor who was attending a party in the Dorchester had saved Elizabeth's life by racing to her suite and pushing a thin plastic tube down her throat before she lost consciousness. He managed to hook her up to an oxygen cylinder and told Eddie that his wife had been fifteen minutes away from death and required an immediate tracheotomy. Eddie didn't know what a tracheotomy was. But next day the whole world and his wife did. The surgical team had cut a hole in her throat to ease the congestion which was choking her. Four times she stopped breathing. Four times she was put into an iron lung. Health bulletins were issued every quarter of an hour. Flowers filled the wards and letters overflowed the hospital's laundry baskets. There was a telegram from Debbie Reynolds and another from the Boeing plant in Seattle saying: 'Six thousand of us are praying for you Liz.' Cleopatra was forgotten. The haggling stopped. Speculation that she was to be replaced by Marilyn Monroe ceased. From Hollywood Skouras cabled: ' Do anything to make Liz happy. She is the only one who matters, the only one who counts.'

Eddie, who was recovering from an emergency appendectomy stayed at her bedside night and day. The Queen's doctor brought in the Queen's portable commode. A special drug (*Staphage Lysate*) was flown in from America. So were her mother and father and her Hollywood physician Dr Rex Kennamer. The life and death drama lasted less than a week and after a final bulletin from London specialist, Dr Carl Goldman, saying: 'Out of every one hundred who have Miss Taylor's type of pneumonia rarely do two survive', this extraordinary movie queen was sitting up in bed sipping champagne.

When she was wheeled out of the hospital a fortnight later wearing a strip of plaster on her neck like another woman would wear a string of pearls, she said: 'This scar is my badge of life. I wear it with pride because it reminds me of the time my life was saved.' The fans cheered and so did her peers when she limped up on the arm of Eddie Fisher, to receive her Oscar from Yul Brynner. Around her ankle was a bandage. It hid, or emphasised, the incision the surgeons had made when she was being fed intravenously on her death bed. The TV camera zoomed onto her badge of life, the bright red scar at the base of the throat. She was no longer the scarlet lady. She was Hollywood's purple heart.

A week later she stood alongside the Attorney General, Robert Kennedy as 'a symbol of the miracle of modern medicine' at a Los Angeles Medical Fund dinner and said: 'Throughout those many critical hours in the operating theatre at the London Clinic, wanting to live was so strong within me — so overpowering, so all-consuming — that I remember it, strangely perhaps, as an incredible and agonising pain. As if every nerve, every muscle, my whole physical being, was being strained to the point of torture — by this insistence upon life, to the last ounce of my strength, to the last gasp of my breath. But then, gradually and inevitably and finally, that last ounce of strength was drawn. I remember I had focused desperately on the light hanging directly above me. It had become something I needed almost fanatically to continue to see; that light had become my vision of life itself. But yet slowly, as if its course of power were my own fading strength and ability to breathe, it faded and dimmed – ironically enough, like a well-done theatrical effect — to blackness. I have never known,

13

nor do I think there can be, a greater loneliness ...
And then I coughed. I moved. I breathed. And I
looked. That hanging lamp — the most beautiful light
my world had ever known — began faintly to glow
again, to shine again.'

Here, with rhetorical excess, was Elizabeth Taylor,
the actress of hyper-sensitive emotions, responding to
a dramatic situation and behaving like the all-time
Hollywood movie star that she was. Little did Senator
Kennedy and the medical men who listened to her
realise that the faint glow from the lamp of their
miraculous symbol was about to burst into a flaming
torch that would scorch the headlines, seemingly
forever more, and fuse together the names of Burton
and Taylor, more solidly in the hearts and minds of the
cinema-going public, than Goldwyn and Mayer and
Antony and Cleopatra.

How the torch came to be lit is a matter that I will
deal with in a personal way later, but it is certainly true
that the greatest revenge of a cuckold was when Eddie
Fisher lost out to Richard Burton, made his wife's
adultery public and let his rival keep his missus. This
was six months after the Cleopatra Circus came to
Rome.

When Elizabeth was giving 'the light of her world'
speech, Burton was giving 'a majestic performance'
(Kenneth Tynan) as 'the magical King Arthur' (*Time*)
in *Camelot* on Broadway. His dressing room
backstage at the Majestic Theatre, known as Burton's
Bar, became the hub of social life, attracting anyone
who was any sort of drinker. It was invariably packed
with actors, agents, secretaries and visiting firemen.
One such visitor was Walter Wanger. He waited for
the crowd of courtiers and agents to disperse and then
accompanied Richard and a leggy blonde chorus girl,

Pat Tunder, to the 21 Club where he outlined plans for the new *Cleopatra*. Fox were willing to pay $50,000 for his premature release from his *Camelot* contract if he was prepared to accept a quarter of a million dollars for three months' work, plus $1,000 a week as living expenses and a villa and staff in Rome for his family. Burton had no hesitation. Wanger liked the look of Pat Tunder and was well pleased when Richard included her in a toast to 'the future'. The cast knew all about Pat. When the chorus sang 'I wonder what the King is doing tonight?' It usually came out as 'It's Tunder who the King is screwing tonight.'

For twelve years Richard had successfully maintained his dual roles in life: the gay, rumbustious extrovert, a hellraiser in the eyes of men, a romantic figure of deadly fascination to women. That he was able to reconcile these two conflicting images was due largely to the exceptional qualities of his wife Sybil. Sharing his Welsh heritage and language, and having been with him from the first day he stepped on to a film set, this beautiful lady with the prematurely silver hair knew and understood him to a remarkable degree. She understood and appreciated his whole *raison d'être* — his inner compulsion to prove himself (to himself as well as others), his instinctive urge to dominate every scene in the life he was playing. More pertinent, she had sufficient wit, intelligence, personality and charm of her own to hold his undiminishing respect and affection. She was more mature than her husband and had the sense to recognise and accept her situation — not grudgingly, but gratefully. She adored him, yet was never absurdly possessive. She was familiar with his dark moods and cheerful indifference, yet never sought to change him. Sybil was quite a personality in her own

15

right. Richard knew it, and their closest friends regarded them as the perfect match. 'They were wonderful together,' said one old friend. 'But perhaps because of her grey hair one tended to see Sybil as mother figure to him.'

This was the background to what was to become the 'most public adultery in the world' when the paths of the principals concerned in *Cleopatra* converged in Rome. Rex Harrison arrived from England to play Caesar. His companion Rachel Roberts went unnoticed. Yet this was the only affair that would end in marriage during the shooting of the film. It also joined the house of Harrison with the house of Burton through Sybil and Rachel's friendship which had blossomed when they shared the same stage as Richard during his 1951 season in Stratford as Prince Hal. Another strong link between the house of Burton and the house of Taylor was Elizabeth's first leading man (or boy as he then was) Roddy McDowall. He played opposite her in *Lassie Come Home* in 1942 and had been bought out of *Camelot* to play the part of Octavius. He was a regular at 'Burton's Bar' and knew all about Pat Tunder and most of the intimate details of Elizabeth's affairs. More than anyone else he knew the true relationship between her and the confused bisexual Montgomery Clift. They were a threesome when her marriage broke up with Hilton and were a threesome again when her relationship with Wilding became that of brother and sister. It was at a party in Roddy's flat that she first met Eddie Fisher, then on leave from the Army, and now her old friend was living in a villa on the Appian Way along with Sybil, the Burton children, Kate and Jessica and his partner in a photographic business. Nearby, at a $3,000-a-month rental, Elizabeth had taken the Villa Papa, a ranch-style house standing in extensive grounds screened by high walls with seven bedrooms and six bathrooms. There she lived with Eddie, her three children, a collie, a St Bernard, three terriers and two Siamese cats. Soon the family was to be increased. On 15 January the Fishers announced that they had adopted Maria Schell, a little German girl who had been found at the age of nine months covered with abcesses, suffering from malnutrition and lying in a laundry basket. Maria, now a year old, had a crippled hip and was entering a Munich clinic for the first of a series of operations.

The scene was set. They started shooting on 25 September, 1961 without a completed script and without Richard. Apart from peeping around pillars now and then he wasn't required for the early scenes between Elizabeth and Rex Harrison. In the first nineteen weeks he did no more than five days' work. There wasn't a whisper of scandal until Elizabeth (as the Queen of fatal fascination who ensnared, weakened and destroyed her lovers) and Richard (as Antony, her last great paramour) played their first scene on 22 January.

Even then the electricity between them, although felt on the set and commented upon by Walter Wanger, was a portrait of themselves as artistes. Richard was in fact suffering from a king-sized hangover and played on Elizabeth's sympathy. 'A slug of whisky,' said he. 'God, no,' said she. She steadied his shaking coffee. He relaxed. She fussed. Later she said: 'He was so vulnerable and sweet. If it had been a planned strategic campaign, Caesar couldn't have done it better. He was captivating. My heart went out to him.'

Whenever it happened, or where it happened,

Richard knew that he had let himself in for more than he had bargained for when Eddie left Rome on 14 February and Elizabeth turned up on the set to watch Richard working. That night they went out on the Via Veneto and were caught in the flashlights of the infamous *paparazzi* — the Italian freelance shutterbugs. Elizabeth was no longer wearing Mike Todd's wedding ring; the twisted and charred relic of the air crash which she swore she would wear forever in memory of her greatest love. When the photographs appeared with question mark captions the studio's American publicity chief, Jack Brodsky, was told by Richard, 'Jack, love, I've had affairs before. How did I know the woman was so fucking famous? She knocks Khruschev off the front page. I just got fed up with everyone telling us to be discreet. I said to Liz, "Fuck it, let's go out to fucking Alfredo's and have some fucking fettucini".' Two days later Roddy McDowall suddenly appeared at the studios to tell Richard that Sybil was packing to leave for America. Elizabeth who was already depressed because Richard was flying to Paris to complete scenes in *The Longest Day* became hysterical when he told her that the romance was over and that Sybil and the children came first. Richard left for the airport and Roddy, Wanger and Mankiewicz were left to comfort their distraught star.

The public were completely unaware of this drama and would have remained so had not Elizabeth taken a few Seconals to make her sleep. Wanger, who was staying at the villa that night, was awakened by the scream of sirens. He came downstairs and was told that Elizabeth had been rushed to hospital. There were rumours of a suicide attempt and the studio put out a food poisoning story, attributing the blame to a tin of bully beef.

Eddie read the story in Milan, Richard in Paris. Both men flew back and the studio panicked. Chris Hofer a publicity man put out a statement in Burton's name denying rumours of a romance. It was published all over the world on 19 February: 'For the past several days uncontrolled rumours have been growing about Elizabeth and myself. Statements attributed to me have been distorted out of proportion, and a series of coincidences has lent plausibility to a situation which has become damaging to Elizabeth. Mr Fisher, who has business interests of his own, merely went out of town to attend to them for a few days. My foster-father, Philip Burton, has been quite ill in New York and my wife Sybil flew there to be with him for a time since my schedule does not permit me to be there. He is very dear to both of us. Elizabeth and I have been close friends for over twelve years. I have known her since she was a child star and would certainly never do anything to hurt her personally or professionally. In answer to these rumours, my normal inclination would be simply to say "No Comment", but I feel in this case things should be explained to protect Elizabeth.'

Next day Burton said he never issued nor authorised a denial of a romance which never existed. 'I have always believed that professional publicity should be kept as far as possible from one's personal life. Now, more than ever before, I believe my reasoning is justified.'

No one was too certain about his personal life, Elizabeth included. She had confessed everything to Eddie Fisher and a week later he threw a thirtieth birthday party for her at the swank Hostaria del' Orso. She seemed radiant and was wearing his birthday present — a $250,000 emerald necklace. Roddy McDowall was a guest. Burton wasn't. He was home with Sybil.

On 1 March, St David's Day, Burton went on an all night bender with Pat Tunder. Whether the presence of the Copacabana showgirl assured Sybil that *the* affair was over, or whether she had completely lost patience with Burton's cheerful indifference to the women in his life, is not known. But on 3 March she flew back to America and left her husband to sort himself out. Two days later during their big *Cleopatra* love scene, Pat was watching on the sidelines. So was Eddie. Later he was to say. 'It wouldn't have mattered if I had sent them an engraved card telling them the time I was coming. They couldn't keep their hands off each other.' It was the last that was heard of Miss Tunder. Elizabeth had given her the message. A few days later Burton gave Eddie the message when he was invited to the Fisher villa to talk things over. Eddie, teetotal for the last time, was confident. Elizabeth was sitting primly with a serious expression and shining eyes. Burton was pixillated. As Eddie was about to speak he put his finger to his lips and said: 'Before you go any further boyo, I think you should know that I'm in love with your girl.' Poor Eddie was left with the music hall cliché of 'That's not my girl. That's my wife.' Burton grinned. 'Well, then, dummy, I'm in love with your wife.' Elizabeth laughed and put her hands to her mouth as Burton turned on her. 'What's so funny fatso. Who do you love?' Elizabeth stood up and didn't look at Eddie. 'You,' she said. 'Right answer,' growled Burton. 'But not quick enough.' Eddie left the room and didn't slam the door. Next day Eddie flew to New York and went into hospital for three days rest.

On 29 March Eddie left hospital suddenly. Elizabeth had asked for a reconciliation after Sybil had arrived in London on her birthday and announced that Elizabeth was her greatest friend. 'I am furious about these rumours, so is Richard, so is Elizabeth,' she said. Eddie called a press conference, and to prove to the reporters that all was well, he offered to get Elizabeth to deny the rumours on the telephone. Poor Eddie proved himself the sucker of the year — the all-time loser. Elizabeth said: 'Sorry, Eddie. I can't tell them that.' The headlines LIZ AND EDDIE TO SPLIT and LIZ TURNS DOWN EDDIE'S OCEAN PHONE CALL brought the world to Rome.

Two days later Emlyn Williams, godfather to the Burtons' first daughter, visited Richard in Rome and left behind an acid letter in which he chastised him and Elizabeth for what he regarded as irresponsible behaviour and expressed the opinion that theirs was an infatuation which could not last. He wrote: 'April 1st, 1962 — known as April Fool's Day. Could it be Richard Burton's year to play the part?'

He told me. 'Sybil is bereft. She really doesn't know what is happening. She's just come from Rome herself and is convinced there is nothing. But a great friend of Sybil's said to me: "If only you could go over and see what is happening." I wouldn't have done so otherwise, because it isn't in my nature to do that sort of thing and I would never do it again. Anyway it is obvious to me. All I have done is to throw them into each other's arms. Richard told me himself, "I'm going to marry her."'

It was the first mention of marriage but not for publication. Later Emlyn Williams told me. 'I came back to England like one of those messengers in a play bring bad news. It was a very bad part I had. Very

21

poor.' Mr Williams had rather overplayed his hand in Rome. He had been reading the Riot Act to Richard when Elizabeth came in and impulsively he said, 'Look at her — she's just a third class chorus girl.' When he got home he told his wife what he had said. Molly Williams drew herself up to her full height. 'Emlyn,' she said haughtily, 'when you met me *I* was a third-rate chorus girl.'

My involvement in *la grande affaire de coeur* at that time was purely incidental curiosity. There were other stories, other showbusiness personalities. Rachel Roberts had married Rex Harrison. Catlin, Dylan Thomas's widow, was living in Rome. Both ladies knew Richard well. Sweet Rachel, now dead, said, 'For Rex's sake I am happy for Richard and Elizabeth. They visit us often. But when they are gone and Rex is asleep, I cry a bit for Syb. She put up with a lot and still does. I think she's marvellous. And to think I used to look at her and envy her happiness. I don't know what's going to happen, but I don't think anything will be the same again.' Catlin, who is Irish, refused to discuss the subject, but she laughed the loudest at *Bricktops* when an American said the Vatican Radio had called the behaviour of Richard and Elizabeth 'an insult to the nobility of the hearth' and she commented 'The shit has really hit the fan.' An Englishman at the bar lowered his glasses and answered: 'Don't you mean the fans have hit the shits.' It seemed that way. There was outrage in America. Ed Sullivan said on television: 'We can only hope that youngsters will not be persuaded that the sanctity of marriage has been invalidated by the appalling example of Mrs Taylor-Fisher and married man Burton.'

It was 1962 and sex outside marriage was still the big

taboo. Southern Congresswoman Iris Blitch claimed in the House of Representatives that Elizabeth Taylor had lowered the prestige of American women abroad and the Attorney General should 'take measures to determine whether or not Miss Taylor and Mr Burton are ineligible for re-entry into the United States on the grounds of undesirability.'

When Fox's School for Scandal broke up forever on 28 July after ten mad months of work and play, Mr Burton and Mrs Fisher packed their bags and went their separate ways. Elizabeth joined Rex Harrison and Rachel Roberts at Santa Margherita on the Italian Riviera. Richard returned to his wife and family in Switzerland. Supreme optimists now saw a distinct chance that the affair might die a natural death, and this might have been just conceivably possible. Instead, however, they were not even separated by frontiers. The Burtons had their villa on the west side of Lake Geneva; Elizabeth now returned to hers on the east side, an hour's drive away by fast car. It was too convenient.

Chapter Two

A YEAR HAD slipped by and the *Cleo* lovers were as isolated by public opinion as Elizabeth and Eddie had been in 1958. They had come to England to play husband and wife in *The VIPs*, an elaborate story of assorted celebrities marooned by fog in London Airport. Away from the set they were playing the same scenario in the VIP suites of the Dorchester. But instead of Elizabeth being cast as the unfaithful wife running away with a lover she found herself in the role of the lover watching the unfaithful husband going home every now and again to the wife and children. In the confusion of his divided emotions and troubled conscience he was drinking so heavily and so consistently that his family feared for his sanity.

One night with Elizabeth and friends in the Dorchester he stood up to recite a piece from Dylan Thomas and vomited over the table. Otto Preminger went to help and Richard made an enemy for life by telling the world famous director and producer to 'fuck off'. On another occasion in mid-January 1963 he was returning from the Wales–England rugby match at Cardiff Arms Park when he was set upon. In explaining an enormous black eye, he alleged that he was looking for a taxi outside Paddington Station when 'I found myself talking to ordinary passers-by —

surrounded by half a dozen Teddy boys. Suddenly somebody started lunging out. Then one got me on the ground. And there you're helpless. They just kicked me all over. One of them put his boot in my eye.' There were many who thought he had been given a 'going-over' by returning fans on the train. A member of the London Welsh told me it wasn't a gang. 'There was an argument in the corridor and this character barged him into the bog, left him sprawled on the lavatory floor and said, "That's where a shit who's done the dirty on his wife deserves to be."'

The criticism of the world he shrugged aside, but not the bitter disapproval of fellow countrymen, particularly his family. Graham, his younger brother, who was the first to make his peace with Richard told me of a night in the Dorchester when he was invited to go out to dinner with Richard and Elizabeth. 'But Richard was missing. I don't know what the hell had happened to him. Elizabeth, as usual had taken ages to get ready, and when she finally made an appearance we had to hang around. It wasn't very nice. He turned up as pissed as a newt, called her some awful names and refused to come out with us. I took her to the dinner on my own. It was obvious that he'd had a bloody great barney with our brother Ivor. At that time Ivor was in Hampstead with Sybil and the children, and Richard worried more about what he thought of him than all the rest of the family put together. In fact, at the beginning of *The VIPs* I stood in as Richard's double for a week so that he could go down to Wales and sort things out with the relations. But all through that film it was a trying time. Ivor was really forceful and sort of inferred that it was either Elizabeth or him. In other words Elizabeth or Sybil.'

But Ivor never had to make the choice. Sybil made

it for him and for Richard too. Her sudden decision to make her home in New York came with the realisation that her acceptance of the role of a second-hand wife would always be paid for in promissory notes. The break-up had already divided their friends into three distinct groups — those who were close to Richard, those who sided with Sybil, and those who remained neutral. But almost everyone, whatever their viewpoint, shared one reaction — astonishment that the separation had ever occurred.

Brook Williams, who remained strictly neutral even though he later offered to marry Sybil, told me: 'I felt sorry for both of them. But I didn't take any side. I felt too many people took sides. Everybody, it seemed, had to be on one side or the other and I thought it was none of our business and presumptuous for anyone except the immediate family to take sides. I know my father did but he had known them both so long that he was regarded as family.'

One who had known them even longer was Stanley Baker. He went to school with Sybil in Ferndale and was Richard's stand-in when he first made his appearance on the professional stage as a boy actor. A rough and lovely man who was knighted and died too young, he said: 'To this day — and I don't give a damn what Richard says — it is extraordinary that their marriage ever broke up. In this superficial world we live in there is so much nonsense talked, so much pretence, and yet here was one girl who had none of that. She was a genuine person with great humour, wit, intelligence and warmth. An attractive woman, a very sexy woman. It seemed they were a perfect match, a perfect foil for each other. Love? I don't know anything about that; it's a purely personal thing. But Elizabeth and Sybil are so diametrically opposed.

And by this time, let's face it, Richard knew a lot about life in this business and must have realised how superficial it is, how long certain things can last, and what your values are. Yes, it is extraordinary that the marriage has broken up, and it shows how wrong you can be about people. I just thought — and it appeared not only to me but to everybody — that Richard and Sybil were two peas in a pod, dead right for each other. They had great warmth and they were wonderful company. They used to sing together and they were like one — they really were. I remember going out to Italy and putting my head on the chopping-block. He said at the time, "Nothing will change the way I feel about Sybil. Nothing will break our marriage," And hell, now they are split up. So something drastic must have happened — in a month, in a day, in an hour maybe.'

Graham Jenkins expressed the belief that, if it were allowed, Richard's solution would have been to have two wives. And some of Richard's friends shared that view. 'I think it's absolutely right that he would have loved to have been married to both of them,' said Robert Hardy, the actor, who met Burton when they were cadets at Oxford. 'I always saw him as a nubile Emperor. But such is the nature of woman that you can't do that. It's the hardest thing to keep a mistress whom you love and to be married to a wife you love. It will never change — such is woman's need and determination to keep monogamous.'

Sybil's virtue, whatever her need, was silence, but even this dignity in the public affair seemed cheapened when she broke her silence and said: 'I would never allow the father of my children to become the fifth husband of Elizabeth Taylor. I'm not going to cut the leash, and when I get him back I'll be two

28

million dollars richer.' Her naming a price in public was seen as a disclosure of Richard's private promissory love notes and confirmed the cynical accusation that Burton was seeking fame and fortune through Elizabeth.

Time seemed to think so when they awarded him their cover-page. They saw him as 'chained in taffeta' at the Dorchester. 'The outcome of the Taylor–Burton game must inevitably yield up a loser. If he should ever marry her, he will be the Oxford boy who became the fifth husband of the Wife of Bath. If she loses him, she loses her reputation as a fatal, an all-consuming man-eater, the Cleopatra of the twentieth century. With or without company, Elizabeth tries to stay close by him twenty-five hours a day, filling poor Richard's almanac with some dull stretches of prose as well as short bursts of poetry.

'In his less insouciant moments, he tears himself to pieces, maddened with guilt. Anonymous, he says, is the word that describes him, for he has given up everything that truly matters to him. Borrowing Keats' epitaph he says again and again, "My name is writ in water." Now that Sybil has gone to New York, he sits quandaried in London. Does he want to be the richest actor in the world, the most famous actor in the world, or the best actor in the world — and in what order? Or just a household word?

'In the short space of a year or so, he has become as well-known as a name can be. Everyone, in short, knows who Richard Burton is, or at least what he is at the moment. He is the demi-Atlas of this earth, the arm and burgonet of men, the fellow who is living with Elizabeth Taylor. Stevedores admire him. He is a kind of folk hero out of nowhere, with an odd name like Richard instead of Tab, Rock, or Rip, who has out-tabbed, out-rocked and out-stripped the lot of them. He is the new Mr Box-Office.'

That Burton was a folk hero, a household word and Mr Box-Office was clearly demonstrated by the unusual advertising for *Cleopatra*. The New York posters merely presenting a giant painting of Elizabeth and Richard and the name of the Rivoli. There was no need to name the film or the stars; their universally recognised faces told it all.

But this fame was chained in taffeta at the Dorchester. Sybil was never to regret her move to New York. No longer living in the shadow, her life changed dramatically. She loved the ballet even more than the theatre, and soon she was engaged in a social life far gayer than anything she had known in Switzerland or even London. She was never alone. She had old friends like Philip Burton and Roddy McDowall, and new ones like Jeremy Geidt of The Establishment satirical group at The Strollers Club.

You can chew over a dilemma for so long. Suddenly there comes a point when it becomes a collosal bore and pales into minor significance. After some uneasy financial months in New York Sybil went into a huddle with Richard's lawyer, Aaron Frosh, stipulating that he deposit one million dollars into her Swiss account and pay her $500,000 a year for the next ten years. Geidt did not give her the usual tea and sympathy routine, but kept plugging the line: 'Well what are you going to do next?' Together they conceived the idea of setting up as a production team and taking over the upper floors of The Strollers Club to open a theatre. She had taste and found she had a flair for casting. As the co-director of The Establishment Theatre Company she was responsible for the off-Broadway production of *The Ginger Man*,

The Knack and *Square in the Eye.*

Later when The Establishment group left New York she took over the The Strollers Club and turned it into the top discotheque of the Western world. She invited her wealthy New York friends to invest in the project. Sammy Davis Junior chipped in a thousand dollars. Sybil named the niterie Arthur, not after Richard's role in *Camelot*, but after the name given to a haircut style by Beatle George Harrison in the film, *A Hard Day's Night*. She then hired a sensational group called The Wild Ones, and almost immediately Arthur's became the most in-place and Sybil the most celebrated hostess in town. She appeared almost daily in the fashion and gossip columns, pictured frugging with Nureyev and hugging every star in town.

Sybil astonished the old friends of her husband with her extraordinary flair, energy and commercial sense and eventually, in June 1965, she was to astonish everybody even more by marrying Jordan Christopher, the young long-haired leader of The Wild Ones. The alliance of thirty-six year old Sybil Burton, the retiring Welsh Methodist wife of the superstar and the mother of his two children, and the twenty-four-year-old Macedonian rock 'n' roller from Arkron, Ohio, shook Richard especially when she gave up her fortune in alimony to marry a man twelve years younger than herself. Afterwards he bought Elizabeth a house in England with the money the remarriage saved him. Elizabeth called it 'Sybil's Folly'. But it wasn't a folly. Sybil prospered and made an entirely new world for herself — with such dramatic change that when she married she was described as 'the white tornado' of the jet-set.

'I admired her tremendously,' Emlyn Williams told me. 'When she married it was very hard to tell which friends were Richard's and which were hers. But you did realise afterwards that they were not just her friends because Richard was a famous actor. They adored her too, and people like Roddy McDowall were marvellous. They stuck by her and were permanent friends. My fear had been that if she were going to make the break she would disappear into the Welsh valleys and become just a sad little lady. But not at all. She had always behaved so beautifully, and it was marvellous that she was to become a great personality on her own. It was a happy ending to a very bumpy journey.'

But that was two years away.

Amazingly, in 1963 no one knew what Burton's intentions really were. At the Dorchester they went through the charade of separate suites, The Terrace and The Harlequin. Even in the 'swinging sixties' the proprieties of society had to be maintained. It didn't matter that Eddie Fisher was advertising their concubinage by appearing with Juliet Prowse, who slinked on stage singing 'I'm Cleo the nympho of the Nile. She uses her pelvis just like Elvis. There was no man she couldn't get — that was Cleo's problem on and off the set.' Elizabeth was still married to Eddie. And Richard was still confusing the public psyche by saying there would be no divorce between himself and Sybil.

Nobody had interviewed them. Everything was supposition until my editor, Howard French, had the bright idea of running a five-part series on the making of *Cleopatra* to coincide with the release of the movie. It was what is called 'a cuttings job' and I was lumbered with it. I had been in Rome covering another non-interview story — the death of Pope John — and French, better known as French Without

32

Leave, gave me a few days off to sort out the saga. I said 'Thanks for nothing.' But little did we realise that French had handed me a world scoop.

I was living in Shepperton at the time and was crossing the road to my local when a Rolls Royce screeched to a halt outside the Anchor Garage making me leap back onto the pavement. The passenger door opened and The O'Toole, Peter himself, stepped out with arms outstretched. In his left hand was a bottle. In the other hand a glass. We sat on the low wall and he poured me a large one. 'You mean you've got to do the same sort of thing as you did with me in *Lawrence of Arabia*?'

'More or less. But that had a bit of life in it, not much I know, but at least I knew you.'

'Well I'm here. So is Richard. It couldn't be easier. I'm playing King Henry to his Saint in *Becket*. Why not talk to him?'

I held out the glass. 'Fat chance. When I was in Rome a year ago I didn't even get a glimpse of them. But at least I saw the Pope.'

'God, aren't you the miraculous one. I thought you were there to cover the funeral.'

'I was, but they let us into the Vatican library and there was little John laid out and all dressed up and everyone genuflecting and kissing his tiny slippers.'

'And did you give him a kiss?'

'For my dear old Irish mother's sake I did; and it wasn't too nice after all those Italian moustaches had slobbered on his toe.'

'That's a great gas. I have an idea. Just kiss the back of me hand and I'll be back.'

'You're pissed O'Toole.'

'And why not.'

Peter marched across the dusty square and

33

disappeared into the King's Head. A few minutes later he reappeared waving his hands. In the back bar was Richard Burton. 'I was wondering when you would turn up,' he said. 'The landlord told us you were living in the village and Peter told me you were an old mate. Did you know we were here?'

'No,' I lied. 'Not until Peter told me he was playing the King opposite you.'

'I'll have to be careful,' said Burton. 'He's already played the ace against me as far as you're concerned. When I kiss Elizabeth I can tell her she has kissed the lips that have kissed the hand that was kissed by the lips that kissed the Pope. I think she'll be curious enough to welcome you.'

Being a journalist is being in the right place at the wrong time and having the luck to be accepted first time.

Chapter Three

MY RELATIONSHIP WITH Richard and Elizabeth during the summer of 1963 in Shepperton was never that of a question-and-answer journalist. It was never that boring and had something to do with the character and personality of the village and its extraordinary population of characters whose eccentricity prompted Richard to describe them as 'actors in search of an author'. Whatever they were in search of they certainly weren't seeking the reflected fame of Richard and Elizabeth.

Archie, the landlord of the King's Head, where we lunched every day, greeted Richard with the immortal line: 'Now is the winter of our discontent made glorious summer by this leg of pork.' He always called Richard 'Master' and Elizabeth 'Mummy'. Maybe it was her generous breasts that reminded him of his wife, Ruth, a gorgeous Edwardian lady bountiful who mothered Elizabeth and had a worldly toleration of the idiosyncrasies of her customers, particularly her husband who was his own best customer.

Elizabeth, sometimes wearing jeans, felt so at ease that she would wander into 'Ma' Rowley's corner shop and buy ice-lollies for her sons Michael and Christopher and any other kids who happened to be there. And little Leslie Rowley, who rarely knew the price of anything, would occasionally knock over a row of canned beans in his excitement. Every day provided such curious distraction that Richard said he was recording it in his diary for an English *Under Milk Wood*.

I took Richard across the square to meet Len, who didn't know Burton from a bar of soap, and had thrown his television set on the Guy Fawkes bonfire in 1953. He ran The Hovel, an ancient restaurant with most things on the slant including himself. He had his appendix on display in a bottle on the bar along with a shunken head and a pickled penis of uncertain age and origin. Richard could never persuade Elizabeth to visit The Hovel which was probably just as well, since she didn't know about the loudspeaker hooked up to the ladies' lavatory and the wind machine that blew up ladies' skirts.

I introduced him to Raymond Ray, a fellow thespian of ancient vintage who wore a monocle, shabby yachting-cap and tatty tennis shoes. He lived in a tea-stained cabin aboard a waterlogged little motorboat on the Thames and told Richard how he once stole one of Lord Beaverbrook's secretaries, along with a motorbike, and put her into an interesting condition on Beachy Head. Ray would kiss Liz's hand like a French count whenever Archie wasn't looking.

There was always another character to delight in a village that considered itself sane and the rest of the world mad. There was for instance the day when Peg Leg, the local rag-and-bone merchant, who wore a belt containing all the regimental cap badges of Britain round his belly, found himself sitting on his bum when his false leg gave way and said: 'Bloody hell, that's the first time it hasn't been able to stand up to eighteen pints.' Richard came in from the back bar and handed Peggy back his leg and called Archie over.

'That fellow you sent through with an impediment. Is he some sort of sex maniac?'

'Old Clefty, a sex maniac! Not him,' said Peggy ignoring Archie and pulling on his leg like Wellington. 'Copped it in the war, didn't he ... got the DSO – dick shot off.'

'But he came in and indicated he wanted Elizabeth's autograph,' said Richard. 'Then when she was about to sign the menu, he pulled out a ball point and said, "No, no this is the best thing for signing my balls."'

Peggy laughed so much that his leg fell off again. Richard held his hands to his head in disbelief. 'Not to worry,' said Archie chuckling through his whiskers. 'the poor chap collects for charity. He gets celebrities to sign cricket bats and things. Here ...' He threw Richard a couple of soccer balls. 'You may as well take them in. Tell Elizabeth he's right. A ball pen is the best pen to sign his balls.'

The incident reminded O'Toole of how he got rid of his stammer and lisp along with his teeth when he was kicked in the mouth while playing fullback for a Navy rugby team against the Swedish police and Elizabeth suddenly said, 'But it's not funny when it happens. I nearly lost my teeth and everybody said Richard had thumped me. Remember Richard. We had gone down to Porto Santo Stefano and we sat eating a bag of oranges when miles away we saw a *paparazzi* lurking in the rocks. That was it. We decided to go back to Rome separately. My driver had to brake suddenly and I was thrown against the plastic ashtray.'

And so it started to come out over a dish of tripe and onions in the backroom bar. For the first time they talked about what it felt like to live through the crazy year of *Cleopatra*.

'It was mad, mad,' said Richard. 'Denials to statements never made. We knew all the jokes — Liz goes for a Burton, Burton Tailoring — the lot. We had it all right up to here. All the time we were shooting the film, but that was forgotten. Not that the script had much to remember as it was always only a page or two ahead of the camera. Poor Joe Mankiewicz was directing all day and writing all night. He had to wear white gloves like a traffic cop because his nerves were in such a state and he had come out in a terrible rash.

'It was a nightmare lit by occasional flashes of happiness. But like a war it's only the good times you remember when you come through. We were hurting a lot of people and we knew it. Christ, you don't eat the forbidden fruit and gob the pips in the public eye. But the gossip didn't help. The rumours were fantastic. We were stranded in them. There was even a housekeeper who sold her key-holing. Anything and everything was believed. There was one marvellous one that I was taking Elizabeth out to cover up the affair that she was really having with Joe. One day on set we sent it up. Joe told the publicity department, "Yes, there's some truth in that. Actually Mr Burton and I are in love and Liz is being used as a front."'

Richard chuckled. He even laughed as Elizabeth recalled the hounding by the *paparazzi*, the Roman shutter-bugs who pursued them by night and day on a scale not even paralleled by the pursuit of Anita Ekberg during the making of *La Dolce Vita*.

'Remember, Richard,' said Elizabeth, 'when the two priests came to the door with cameras under their cassocks. And that one the kids called "Creeper". You can laugh now, but he followed us everywhere.

He was a funny little squirt, never a smile. One day I was out with the children picking those beans; you know, the little green ones that grow wild and you eat with cheese. I was just in a pair of old jeans and a shirt, looking a bit of a mess, when one of the kids shouted out: "There's Creeper!" And sure enough, there he was hiding behind a bush. It was the last straw. I went up to him smiling, and swearing through my teeth. He just stood there the dope. Then I grabbed his camera. And *wham*. I clocked him one. But he was back next day. The children, Michael, Christopher and Liza, were chasing him. I think they became rather fond of Creeper.

'You know, you would never believe what went on with those *paparazzi*. They even had a girl on the set walking around with a camera hidden in her top-knot. If you came down in the middle of the night, there would be a blinding flash of light. It got so that you'd sneak around opening every cupboard before you took a bath. They were a bloody nuisance.'

'I remember another time,' said Burton, 'when I was waiting for Liz at the bar of a night club. She came in, saw all those photographers, and burst into tears and ran. I did not even see her. Didn't know she was there. I'm sitting like a muggins while she's being chased. Next day of course there are pictures of Elizabeth running, and I'm supposed to have beaten her up again.'

It wasn't exactly world shattering stuff. But it was first hand. I was getting to know them. Then suddenly came gloom and depression. *Cleopatra* was unveiled at a New York première. Elizabeth, who had more confidence in the film than Richard had, was shattered by the reviews.

Judith Crist in the *New York Herald Tribune*

reported: '*Cleopatra* is at best a major disappointment, at worst an extravagant exercise in tedium. All is monumental, but the people are not. The Mountain of Notoriety has produced a mouse.' Generally the critics raved about Harrison and were reasonably impressed with Burton. The acid was reserved for Elizabeth. She was lacerated.

Crist led the way: 'She is an entirely physical creature, no depth of emotion apparent in her kohl-laden eyes, no modulation in her voice that too often rises to fishwife levels. Out of royal regalia, in negligée or *au naturel*, she gives the impression that she is really carrying on in one of Miami's Beach's more exotic resorts.'

They came with rocks in their hands and they didn't leave a turn of Elizabeth unstoned. 'Overweight, overbosomed, overpaid and undertalented, she set the acting profession back a decade,' said David Susskind. 'When she plays Cleopatra as a political animal,' said *Time*, 'she screeches like a ward heoler's wife at a block party.' 'Miss Taylor is monotony in a slit skirt,' said the *New Statesman*, 'a pre-Christian Elizabeth Arden with sequinned eyelids and occasions constantly too large for her.'

'Despite her great beauty,' said *Cue*, 'Miss Taylor simply does not possess the emotional range — in voice control or movement — to match consistently the professional perfection of Rex Harrision, superb as Caesar, or Richard Burton as the tempestuous, passionate and utterly tragic Antony.'

Richard shouldered his way through a crowd of reporters in Park Lane and gave one quote to a voice that said: 'Harrison did all right then.' The reply was in all the papers next day. In America it was reported as 'Richard Burton says Rex Harrison played Caesar like a draper's clerk.' What he actually said was: 'Rex Harrison is a good actor. I'm pleased for him. It was a great role. He couldn't do wrong in the part; even a draper's clerk could play it.'

When I met Richard in Archie's for lunch, he said, 'Isn't that typical? Look, do us a favour, will you? You know what Elizabeth and I really think about Rex. So just for the record, you know, if you could squeeze it in somewhere that Elizabeth and I think Rex was brilliant. He is an extraordinary craftsman. Great style. There's no sour grapes. I'm just trying to protect Elizabeth. She's been kicked in the teeth. It hurts. I understand it in a way. After all those years and all that ballyhoo — the biggest, the greatest, et fucking cetra, et fucking cetra — it's all too human for critics to say, "Right, let's see if they were worth it." The *New York Times* called them "sceptics predisposed to give Cleopatra the needle."

'I go along with that. And I go along with their critic who says her portrayal of Cleo is one of force and dignity with all the impressive arrogance and pride of an ancient queen. Of course, I'm protective towards Elizabeth. I love her. And she's a great actress. I'll tell you. Whatever else she revealed to me on that film she revealed more about movie acting than I had picked up in every other film I appeared in.'

A few weeks later *Cleopatra* arrived in London. It had been pruned by twenty-two minutes, but still some critics found it a gruelling experience to sit through. We were in Archie's and suddenly Elizabeth exploded. When Crist wrote about Liz's voice often rising to 'fishwife levels' she was probably writing from personal experience. Elizabeth in full screeching throttle would make your everyday foul-mouthed fishwife throw her petticoat over her head in embarrassment. My casual remark that theirs was a classic case to support the cynical argument that publicity, however bad, however distorted, could be advantageous and that the private lives of film stars, exposed mostly by hired press agents, was in the public domain, had set her off. When I pulled her up and reminded her that although I didn't mind her unfounded conviction that my father hadn't married my mother, I did take exception to her charge that I had had sexual intercourse with my mummy.

Her eyes blazed with violet and violent electricity, but before she could spark again, Richard wagged his finger. 'We'll have no more of that mother effing. You'll be giving a bad impression. Pour out the wine, there's a love. Of course, there's publicity — and publicity. Good and bad. It's necessary and I don't knock anyone for doing his job. Let's face it. What do I read on a Sunday? What's the first thing I turn to? Bad publicity for the Government and fascinating reading for millions. Of course I read the Profumo affair and every word about Christine Keeler. Who doesn't?

'And who didn't read all about us? About Liz and myself? You can't be sanctimonious about things until you have read them. That's the fun about being sanctimonious; you have to have expert knowledge before you condemn.'

And then, quite casually, he looked straight into Elizabeth's eyes and said: 'I want to marry Elizabeth, and I will marry her. There have been all kind of rumours but that is what is going to happen. No ifs. No buts. She wants to marry me. I want to marry her.'

Elizabeth dressed all in turquoise clapped her hands to her face. 'You've said it Richard.' She looked at me. 'And you've sent it Western Union. I LOVE

YOU.' She kissed Richard. She kissed O'Toole and she gave me back my kiss from the Pope.

'That's enough of that, Taffy Taylor,' said Richard. 'I think we should drink on this. Scotch?'

'No,' said Elizabeth. 'Champagne. Nothing but champagne will do.'

So at last it was confirmed — firmly, officially, exclusively. I broke the news. The lead-in to my five-part series on *Cleopatra* was a front page splash and it was flashed around the world.

The speculation and conjecture was at an end, and in Shepperton at least the gossiping died down until a few weeks later when Britannia, a local lady of vast surround, came into Archie's and said: 'Haven't you heard? Haven't you read? Burton has never slept with Elizabeth Taylor. Honest! It's all in the papers. And he says she's got short legs, a double chin and too big a chest.'

What she was talking about was the topic of the day for morning coffee parties — the things Richard had said to Ken Tynan in an interview for *Playboy* magazine and now picked up with glee by every newspaper.

Most especially the housewives were intrigued by Richard's dogmatic reference to monogamy being absolute imperative. 'It's the one thing we must always abide by. The minute you go against the idea of monogamy, nothing satisfies anymore. Suppose you make love to a woman — which is exciting in itself. Suppose you make love to her twice, thirty times, forty times. It can't be enough just to go to bed with her. There has to be something else. Something more than absolute compulsion of body.

'Sexually, the relationship may cease but you must never move outside it. If you have an imaginative spouse you may find other solutions, but certainly you mustn't violate the idea of monogamy. If you do, it destroys you. It's a killing process and it shouldn't be encouraged. Love and sex are part of the same thing. Sex alone is utterly unimportant anyway. If one's involved purely sexually, with somebody else — whether it's a man or a woman or a swan — and that makes you deviate from your ideas of absolute right and wrong, then there's something intensely wrong with that involvement. That doesn't mean that you should not leave your wife. If you have to go, go. But don't keep skipping back and forth. You can't use sex as a crutch to get away from her — a kind of moral intellectual psychic crutch. You can't say to her: "I'm terribly sorry, but I can't sleep in the same bed with you any more because I simply *have* to go off with this infinitely more fascinating girl." There is no such thing as a more fascinating girl. They are all the same, and our appetites are all the same. Sex is no excuse. There is no excuse for infidelity.'

Well!

At the studios, dressed as the saintly *Becket*, Richard rubbed his hands over his face and slapped his forehead. 'Don't tell me. They've been sending me up all morning. O'Toole has been reading the story out to me and asking what it means. And Elizabeth has been on the phone.'

I looked at him. He was the true egoist. Conscious of the divine spark of his nature. Telling things that are true of himself and no one else. He smiled back.

'There's no confusion. That's why I told you I'm going to marry Elizabeth. I'm not skipping back and forth. Did I say it? You know me by now. Of course I did. It was an interview at the Dorchester that lasted six hours and six bottles with Tynan's tape recorder

44

going the whole time. I dictated enough to make *Gone With The Wind* look like a slim volume of verse. I'm a confusion of talk. For instance, I heard myself saying on one part of the tape: "Good writing is for the minority, because the minority are the only ones who can judge." And then later I heard myself saying: "Good writing can only be judged by the number of people who read it. The more who read it the better it is." But when she comes down later, do me a favour. No cracks about that double chin and the short legs.'

Elizabeth arrived with her three children, Michael, Christopher and Liza and tucked my arm in hers. 'Honestly, you wouldn't believe it. When I came out of the hotel there were photographers waiting to see if they could get a shot of Richard and myself having a punch-up. Really! I don't know what they expect to see — tears streaming down my face? A black eye? Of course I'm not mad with Richard. I love him and I'm going to marry him. It's just that he suffers from this intoxication of words. It's Welsh verbal diarrhoea. But he is so full of shit that I'm not going to let him get away with it. When he comes off the set, pretend that I've made some monstrous statement about him. And keep hold of me. I do love him. I do.'

Michael, aged nine, and always protective towards his mother and younger brother and sister, looked up and said, 'Who do you love Mummy?'

'Richard, darling. I said, I loved Richard.'

He looked at me. 'And I do too Mummy. I love him very much.'

They had now finished the scene in which O'Toole as King Henry tells Becket that he is going to be Archbishop of Canterbury. Richard came over and tossed Liza into the air. His green eyes flickered warily to Elizabeth and myself, and Elizabeth looked

45

up at the sky, whistling through her teeth. Very formally I asked him to comment on a statement by Miss Taylor that he was a bible-black, lying Welsh git. Richard held up his hand and cocked his head in a crafty schoolboy grin. 'It's no good old love. It's no good. I can read her face and that so-called whistling is supposed to be Beethoven's Fifth. It's our special signal and means all is peace. Doesn't she look lovely though? Suit you marvellously those pants, girl.'

'Yes I wore them just for you,' she replied with a Welsh accent. 'Thought they would please you. Show off my short legs to advantage like. Lovely I look, isn't it. Indeed to goodness and all that old bullshit.'

Richard laughed. 'Did you see that now poor old Stephen Ward is dead, we've been promoted to the front page again.'

His pronouncement on monogamy didn't seem to worry Elizabeth and didn't particularly puzzle friends who knew him well. Like so many of his arguments it was Jesuitical, devious and slightly puritanical. Without being at all religious in the conventional sense, he is a man with an acute and profound awareness of sin which he calls guilt. Similarly he feels sinfulness in being a capitalist and guilt about being a socialist only at heart, and because of these conflicts he prefers, like an officer in the Mess, not to become involved in discussions about naming ladies, politics or religion.

Considering that *Becket* brought so many talents together, including Sir John Gielgud as the King of France, the end product proved faintly disappointing. Midway, it appeared to sag and lose pace. Certainly in the transfer from the intimacy of the theatre to the spectacle of the wide screen, Anouilh's central theme of the conflict between Church and Crown dividing spiritual brothers somehow became less compelling. Yet *Becket* gave just the right kind of boost to Burton's prestige. And as Richard triumphed with the critics, Elizabeth purred. She had been absolutely right in her insistence that he, the public sinner, should play the saint.

One night we were sitting in the Dorchester and his eyes rolled back to his childhood. He tried to focus and pointed. 'Irishman, whatever you are. There's nobody like us, I tell you. Look at me, Irishman. In the Miner's Arms on a Saturday night my father would fix his stupendously stoned eyes on his fellow miners and say in Welsh: '*Pwy sy' fel ni?*' And they would answer, '*Neb.*' Then he would intone: '*Pwy sy' fel fi?*' and back would come the chorus voice. '*Neb.*''

He closed his eyes and gave the answers and questions in English, whispering loudly, 'Who is like us?' 'Nobody.' 'Who is like me?' 'Nobody.'

He fell silent and looked at a picture hanging on the wall. 'See that, Irishman. Quarter of a million dollars. Elizabeth bought me that. A Van Gogh. Pictures. I look at them. Schoolboy days in the waxed museum of Wales. Roaming the lost summer days deafened by education. Lend an ear Van. I see only what I see. *Pwy sy' fel ni?*'

I left him asleep. I had a few weeks' holiday coming. I decided to go to Wales to find out what he was like. It was through curiosity rather than biography that I made the journey.

Chapter Four

THE MINER'S ARMS is the only public house in Pontrhydyfen and its name is the only hint that this nondescript straggle of higgledy-piggledy houses on the road to Neath had anything to do with coal mining. Yet this pub, just up the road from where Richard was born Jenkins on 10 November 1925, remains the heroic and sentimental centre of Burton's Welshness and the heaven that lay about him in his infancy. It was from here, on Christmas Eve 1900, that his mother, Edith, a seventeen-year-old barmaid, married her best customer, Tiny Dic, a twenty-four-year old face worker.

They wed without preacher at the registry office in Neath and both signed the register — the first sign of literacy in the history of both families. It was from here that Richard's grandfather, Tom, was carried out paralytic after blowing his winnings on a horse called Black Sambo. The colliers, straight from the pit with their lips washed cherry red from Tom's beer, propped him up in his wheelchair to roll him home. But he released the brake, and with the miners cheering him on, he charioted down the hill, beating the air with an imaginary whip, and yelling: 'Come on my son! Come on Black Sambo!' They were his last words. He crashed into a wall and was killed instantly.

It was all here. It was here that Richard's father celebrated the births of his thirteen children, mourned the deaths of his wife and two of his daughters and finally — and inevitably since he rarely went elsewhere — downed his last pint.

And it was here I pushed open the door and took my first look at what Richard had described as 'the men of my childhood: the salt of the earth'.

The scene wasn't exactly as he painted it 'coal grimy men from the bowels of the earth with teeth that smile like blackamoors.' But most of the ancient regulars wore the blue tattoo of coal scars on the backs of their hands and I could feel the curiosity of their silence as I examined the photographs on the nicotine-stained walls — row upon row of sepia rugby teams, all alike with different dates, but always the same shuffle of fifteen names with initials to distinguish a Davies from a Davies, an Edwards from an Edwards, an Evans from an Evans, a Jenkins from a Jenkins.

'Was it true that Richard Burton played in the same youth team as Gerwyn Williams?' I asked

'Not here he didn't,' volunteered one old miner. 'Born just down the road he was, but never lived here really. Old Jenk's son. Now there's a character if ever there was one. Dic! Wicked little bugger. Isn't that right Bryn? Used to sit over by there near the fire. Christ almighty, old Dic-bach-y-saer.'

'Aye,' said Bryn Davies. 'Dic-bach-y-saer means Richard, the son of a carpenter. I remember him telling me one time that his father was a roofer at the coalface. He'd put in the timber props, you know, when they were cutting the seam. That's how his legs were buggered up when the roof fell in. But little Dic was a sweet man. Only this size, tiny, couldn't be five-two in his boots. But drink! Duw. Bloody hollow legs he had. Wouldn't come up to a big man's shirt button standing on his toes but size is nothing hereabouts. Look around you and you can't imagine what it was like when Richard was born. No pit head baths, you get me, and this place packed with miners soaked to the skin. You'd have to work with the pick, hacking on your side in six inches of freezing water, with only a two foot clearance above you. Significant.'

Bryan tapped his nose. 'The smaller you were, the harder you worked. I think that's where the phrase "cut you down to size" comes from. Stands to reason doesn't it? If you couldn't take a man on down there you couldn't take him on upstairs. Take rugby. All the generals are little men. Dic knew that. So did his sons. Bloody good face workers they were too. In fact Richard, who never went down the pit, was going to buy a mine for them years ago. That's a fact. Anyways, in those days before the war, there were pubs all over the valley. Up here was the Heart of Oak, then the Boar's Head, two others that were a bit of a step, and this place. It was a whitewashed pub then with just one toilet — three walls around, you know, couldn't hold two exactly. Take it in turns to piss out the back. The drinking was tremendous and cheap. No ladies' loo. No need was there? They wouldn't be seen dead in here. You get me. Significant. There were only two ways of life. You were either going to the chapel or the pub, and most of the miners went to the pub, and the women understood because miners' work is hell. But the Calvanistic Methodists were very strong here, exceptionally strict. If a girl got herself in the pudding club she was out. Sent away from the village altogether. Denounced by name in the chapel. That was the accepted thing. No miner would argue. On a

Sunday as a boy you couldn't even use scissors to cut your nails. And the deacons of the church. Duw, boy, you were mortally afraid of them. See one coming. Run and hide. The men of the ministry are practically actors and we thought Richard would be one. But he knew better. They had a tremendous influence. Tremendous! The Welsh gift of language is a sad gift of God — he inclined us all towards poetry and then buried us in coal.

'Dic-bach-y-saer was agnostic. All the women without exception were chapel, and all the children had to go to Sunday school. The fathers would kick their arses out of the house; older ones as well. Stands to reason if you think; only time a husband and wife could be alone. Look at these houses. Three bedrooms at the most; nine children always at least.

'When Richard was only a baby there was the General Strike and there were sixty-six collieries in these parts and twenty-one of them had already been closed because of the Depression and import of cheap Polish coal. At that time it was the most revolutionary place on earth. You can imagine, with fourteen thousand miners doing bugger-all and helpless for their families and not getting enough food for their children and threatened by the bloody army. We marched to London — two hundred miles on the boot. Remember it like yesterday. I was in Charing Cross Road looking for them. "They've been this way boys," I cried. "Look at the gob." The miner's trademark — a trail of yellow and black, and specks of red. Terrible year. We had TB in the wallpaper. Soup kitchens in the street. See a sheep on the mountain. Ten minutes later in the fucking pot, head and all. No messing. No mention in the papers though. All Tory, owned by the same gang that controlled the mines.

There were miners humping their children in little white coffins on their backs. No photography. No telephones. No television. Not even wireless.'

Outside the Miner's Arms the blue Thomas Brothers bus waits to take on passengers going two miles south to Cwmavon, the first village of the Afan valley, or on down to the sprawling steel-town of Port Talbot. The first stop is in the hallow of Pontrhydyfen, hard by number two Dany-y-bont. It was there, in 1928, that sister Cissie lifted two-year-old Richard aboard the bus and took him to live with her miner-husband Elfed James in Taibach, adjoining Port Talbot.

Across the road and a little way up the hillside, Mrs J.E. Jones opens the door to her old stone cottage and asks me in. 'Will you have a cuppa tea? Just wet it this moment.' She chats amiably, offering bakestones and salty butter. The sitting room looks straight onto the street — a grate full of coal and hob with a singing kettle, coconut matting on polished linoleum and on the sideboard a ticking clock and oval photographs of Kitchener moustaches and watch-chains.

'Now I tell you, Richie used to play on that very mat as a baby. And when his mother used to bring him over here she would sit on that very chair. Oh, a lovely woman. I was just married and didn't know how she coped. A lot younger than her husband, but a good bit taller. Dic practically lived in the Miners. Easy going like. Now Mrs Jenkins was very different. Took in washing she did and brewed herb beer in the copper. Used to sell it in old pop bottles. They used to live back there in Station Road. They moved across there to Dany-y-bont when Richie was born. He was the twelfth and weighed twelve pounds — a real whopper! Then about a year later Mrs Jenkins couldn't believe she was having another baby. She said to me sitting right there in that chair. "God almighty, another mouth to feed!" That baby Graham it was, done for her. Forty-five she was. I think it was club money they buried her on. Only one of them left in the village now. Hilda. Sweet woman. Number four Penhydd Street. Up there above the cemetery.'

The old villagers can never forget the appalling poverty of the twenties and thirties. But Hilda looks back on these days with glowing affection.

'I was eight when Richard was born and I can only remember the happy times — like the summers that always seemed long. We were poor and many, but nothing extraordinary. There was a family up the road with twenty-one children, another with eighteen. What's the family now? Well, starting with Tom. He is the oldest and was born in 1901 and has one daughter. Then there's Ciss (Cecilia) who has two girls and Ivor (he died in March 1972, aged sixty-three) with no children. Then comes Will with two children, David with one, Verdun with two and myself with four. I've got the biggest family of the lot. After me is my sister Catherine with three, and my youngest sister Edith who had three children and is now dead. Then of course there is Richard with his daughters Kate and Jessica, and then the very last and youngest, Graham, who has two sons.

'But when we were children I can never remember going without. The house was always happy. In the kitchen we had two tables — one square and one round, with scrubbed tops. All the children under fourteen had to sit at the round table. My father Daddy Ni always had us in fits. He loved his drink. Loved it. We idolised him because there was nothing nasty, ever. I can see my mother laughing at his stories now, and Richard in his arms looking nearly as big as Daddy Ni. And then it was all heartbreak. We were all so happy for Richard to have a little brother and then — my God! Mam was dead. I was the eldest girl at home and only nine. It was like a bad dream. Tom took Graham to live with him at Cwmavon and Ciss took Richie to Taibach. A lot of children in Cwmavon thought that Tom was Graham's father. But different it was for Richard. He had no English and spoke all Welsh to my sister, while her husband Elfed always spoke English. So you can imagine how strange it was for Richie. It was like going to a foreign country.'

Foreign it was. Foreign it still is. I had asked Richard where he would like to be if the world had only thirty minutes to run. Without hesitation he answered: 'Up on The Side, with the old miners and the tinplate workers, squatting one-kneed around a fire and telling yarns and peeling the sooty skins off finger-burning baked potatoes. Up there with the children of my childhood. The men of my childhood.'

The Side — it has no other name — is just the side of a grass mountain leaking coal juice into the gutters and curtaining off the fag-end of Port Talbot in an untidy bundle of terraced side streets called Taibach.

It was here, sandwiched between mountain and sea, his childhood memories began. Elfed James, his brother-in-law (now dead) became his new father but was the exact opposite to Daddy Ni. Richard loved Cissie as a mother but could never accept the tee-total Elfed as a father. Indeed there were, and still are, members of the James family who criticised the Jenkinses for having thrust such a responsibility on a young, meagrely paid miner. While Elfed had the unrewarding task of providing for the boy's basic needs, along with that of his two daughters. Dic-bach-y-saer, released from his parental obligations, could assume a grandfatherly image and spoil his visiting son with occasional gifts. As far as he was concerned it was a natural arrangement. Elfed's mother was his wife's sister. By the rough standards of The Side Richard was quite the privileged boy. He wore shoes. He had roller skates with ball bearings — and a bicycle.

Stanley Baker, now dead and more about him later, was having a tougher, more austere life across the hills in the Rhondda Valley. He told me: 'To have shoes instead of boots was the subtle difference between butter and margarine. It didn't give you any more muscle, but it gave you a shade of class. Let's face it, Richard was bloody lucky with two fathers and five brothers down the pit.

'But if you had one father who'd lost his leg in the mine, like I did, and brothers still at school, then you were a Means Test family. I dressed in the uniform of the poor — head shaved like a convict with a clump of fringe in front, grey jersey made of steel wool, and sturdy short trousers with bloody great patches, and boots — those bloody great clodhoppers, always a size too large.'

There were boys like Stanley in Taibach, but not too many. But there were plenty of teachers like Glyn Morse, who encouraged Baker to become an actor, and Miss Sarah Grace Cooke, who recognised the genius of Emlyn Williams among the dusty chalk rows of her pupils. Two of these dedicated teachers shaped Richard's destiny — Meredith Jones and Philip Burton. He took the name of the latter but it was the former he eulogized when he was invited by the *Sunday Times* to contribute to a series in which distinguished men and women recalled people who changed the course of their lives. He described

56

Meredith Jones as 'a recognisable spiritual descendant of Geraldus Cambrensis and Shakespeare's Fluellen: passionate, fluent, something of a scholar, mock-belligerent, roughly gentle, of remarkable vitality and afraid of nobody. He was the concentrated essence of a kind of bi-lingual South Walian, unknown perhaps over the border, who speaks the alien English tongue with a loving care and octosyllabically too.'

Meredith had long departed when I tracked down his stage — Eastern Boys School — just a walk across the footbridge of the tiny Dyffryn railway that ran below the backgarden of 73 Caradoc Street where Richard lived.

But not everyone remembers Meredith Jones with such exaltation. Gerry 'Luther' Lewis, a classmate of Richard and now a Taibach teacher and professional football referee says: 'Jones had certain qualities — fair do's. But I didn't like him. He was quick with his lip and a bloody sight quicker with the fist. Wonder was that nobody filled him in.

'You see he ran the scholarship class. You got to him when you were ten and sat this monstrous national examination when you were eleven. If you failed you stayed on at Eastern School until you were fourteen and then went into the steelworks or down the mine. No chance. But if you passed you went to Port Talbot grammar or secondary until you were sixteen with university to follow if you were exceptional. Now the difference between a grammar school boy and an elementary was the difference between officers and other ranks. Well there would be thirty-odd children in a scholarship class and in theory the odds of them getting into the grammar were about six to one against. But Jonesie had the highest pass record in the area. And why? Because he handpicked the clever little buggers and ignored the dumb ones.

'I got there without his help and that's when I really got to know Richard. But even then Meredith Jones ran the Taibach Youth Club at night and had his chosen boys following him around the streets. Bar Richard, they were right, regular arse-hole creepers. Do anything he asked. I remember we were playing Neath. Unbeaten at the time. All we had to do was throw the ball about and we were there. But no. Mered was running up and down the touchline shouting, "Keep it tight, boys, keep it tight." And Richie, the skipper and a bloody good loose forward, knew he was wrong but made us keep it tight. We lost 6-3. No, I didn't like Jones. It wasn't jealousy or anything. I just felt it was disgraceful the way he treated boys who were not in the magic circle. I can see him now, striding along with his mac flapping and waving his arms and his tribe following him like he was Jesus. I thought he was slightly off the latch.'

Charles Hockin, also a Taibach schoolmaster, was top of the class at Eastern in Richie's day. But he declined his first chance of going up into the scholarship class because of his distaste for Meredith Jones. 'He was a slave-driving teacher. He used the cane regularly, and you sat there afraid to bat an eyelid in case it rattled. You did nothing else except English and arithmetic with him and the period of joy was once a week when he took Welsh in another class and we had Tom Howell who read us *Night Must Fall*. You either hated Mered or detested him. He had the gift of gab all right, and if you wanted a fellow who was verbose and could step in front of five hundred people and hold them — then, yeah, this was the fellow. But he wasn't a great man to me. To most of us he was a bully of a man.

'He took rugby at the school, and if you couldn't play rugby you were no bloody good for anything. He drove everybody. He bristled. He had a ginger moustache and this purple temper. We had the rudiments of rugby in Mered's class. You went out in the yard and the touchline was a wall. I remember the ball being kicked out and there was this savage horde descending upon me, and because I was near the wall I stepped to one side — discretion being the better part of valour. Well, Mered just blew the whistle and said, "You should have taken that ball, boy." And I said, "But the wall, sir." And then he stood me in the middle of the yard with eight boys in front of me and he kicked the ball up in the air and said, "Right". And as I took the ball I fell back three times, not once, and I was flattened into the ground. Nowadays, as teachers, we would never do anything like that by a wall because we would be afraid of claims and all sorts of things against us. But in those days it was different. You didn't go home and complain to your father about him because you were mortally afraid of the fellow.'

Whatever the personal failings of Meredith Jones, whatever the injustices of his private form of educational separatism, he is still remembered in Taibach as a mover of mountains whose drive and leadership made Taibach Youth Centre the most widely known and respected club in Glamorgan, a prototype for the hundreds now scattered around the country. The wizardry of his words lit fireworks off the penny-comic candles of their minds. And no one was going to be more dramatically influenced than Richie Jenkins.

Yet, oddly enough, when Richard left Meredith's

scholarship class for higher education at Port Talbot Secondary School he seems to have fallen into some kind of limbo. In fact his first stage role in a term-play didn't come until his fourth year. He played the minor of role of veteran ambassador — Mr Vanhattan — in Shaw's political comedy *The Apple Cart*. He made no impression and members of the cast have little or no memory of his stage debut.

Susie Preece, who was his sweetheart for a while, played the part of the Queen. She told me: 'Richie didn't do much in the play as I remember. It was the boy who played the king who we all thought was great. Morgan Griffiths was his name. He had the star part and he was very good. But Richie was just another one of the boys then — quiet, not spectacular. I remember he used to fool about a bit during Welsh. Otherwise he was quite an ordinary boy. I don't think Philip Burton noticed him.'

It was doubtful that he did. Mr Burton, who had come to Taibach straight out of a university with a double honours degree in pure mathematics and history, was a bachelor obsessed by the theatre. Like Meredith Jones he had his magic circle of boys. But unlike the exuberant wordsmith, he was an introvert and looked upon as mildly eccentric by his colleagues.

He had, what he has since called 'this Pygmalion complex', a compelling urge to establish a close personal identification with a pupil and the desire to fulful his own acting ambitions through that person. He didn't see that person in Richard. There were other pupils of obvious flair to follow in the footsteps of his protegé Thomas Owen-Jones, a handsome boy who had won the Leverhulme Scholarship at the Royal Academy of Dramatic Art and had made his film debut in *The Four Feathers*. More to Mr Burton's liking were the well-spoken Hubert Clements of Aberavon and little Hubert Davies who lived just around the corner from Richard in Brook Street.

If Richard entertained thoughts of becoming an actor when he celebrated his sixteenth birthday in 1941 his dreams were shattered that Christmas when Elfed decided it was time his cuckoo nephew earned his own keep. He got him a job serving behind the counter of the men's outfitting department of the Taibach Co-operative Wholesale Society and left Richard stranded without his school certificate which he was due to take the following summer.

Richard says he left 'because I had a wild ambition to go out into the world and starve'. Hilda told me: 'Really and truly he hated that job. He only went there because Cissie's husband was out of work and they were a bit hard up. You know how things were in those days — someone had to go to work. Well, Richard detested it more than anything else in the world. He used to come and tell me. "I hate that bloody job." And the things he did were worrying. There was clothes rationing, and when an old miner came in wanting a suit, Richard would give it without taking coupons. Of course Cissie was terrified.'

Besides the family, only one other person was concerned about Richard: Meredith Jones. He couldn't believe that one of *his* Eastern scholarship boys was condemned to dead-end dealing in men's long-johns.

From the day he barged into the Co-op and found Richard behind the counter he worked for his return to school. Richard had to give him ammunition by demonstrating that he merited treatment as 'a special case'. And Richard provided it by throwing all his spare-time energies into the activities of the Youth

Centre. It was here he met Leo Lloyd who had been invited by Meredith Jones to take charge of the drama group and enter them for the first Youth Eisteddfod to be held at Pontypridd in June 1942. Lloyd responded by calling together five boys and two girls to prepare a production of *The Bishop's Candlesticks* — a mime adaptation of Victor Hugo's *Les Miserables*. Richard played the convict.

Evan Morgan, once one of Philip Burton's star pupils rated Leo as 'one of the most dedicated producers I've met in twenty-five years of professional broadcasting'.

Charles Hockin told me: 'Leo was the original thespian. Tall and all nose and Adam's apple. I can see him now — walking the pavements of Taibach in his large velour trilby, completely oblivious to passers-by, with his head buried in a book and throwing his arms about as he spoke his lines. If you didn't think, eat, speak and live every moment for drama, you were no use to Leo. When the day of the Eisteddfod drew near he was worried about giving the play a real try-out on a real stage which we didn't have. As usual Mered found a way. 'Build a stage from tables and blackboards and we can use the school desks.' But the trial performance was almost ruined when the combined weight of the cast cocked up the blackboards. The rest of us club members were made to crawl under the desks and support the blackboards with our backs. You can literally say that Richard Burton started his acting career on the broad of my back. And we took first prize. I don't care what they say about Phil Burton, I don't think Richie would have got on the roll of honour for anything if it had not been for Mered and Leo.'

By the end of that summer Meredith Jones had

rubbed it into everyone concerned — relatives, local dignitaries and teachers — that here was a boy of exceptional scholastic potential. Most important of all Mered persuaded County Councillor Llewellyn Heycock, a Governor of Port Talbot Secondary, to use his wide powers to have Richard re-admitted to school in September 1942. He also made sure that Philip Burton knew all about the saga of the Jenkins family. The two teachers were fellow officers in 499 Squadron of the A.T.C.

Chapter Five

PHYLLIS CATHERINE DOLAN, the only other pupil in Richard's class to take up acting as a career, remembers his return to Port Talbot Secondary vividly. 'All the girls were terribly excited and there was endless whispering — "Have you heard, have you heard Richie Jenkins is coming back?" Funnily enough, I couldn't place him at all, which was odd because I am related to the James family and had vague recollections of having met him as a child in Cissie's house. But I was as intrigued as the rest because it was quite unique for a boy to leave school for a year, go to work, be seen around town pubbing and that, and then come back as a pupil. And his entrance that day was fantastic. He opened the door and hurled a gym-shoe right across the class and smashed a pane of glass. So Richard was back. And you can imagine the effect on us girls. He was such an attractive young man. Extraordinarily so. And despite his mass of pimples and acne, and those boils on his neck, he even had nicknames for them, no other boy had a chance from that day on. He'd cock those green eyes and it was obvious that no girl would ever hold him. The first day during the break he asked me to go to the pictures and I turned him down because I was going with a boy called Roy Jenkins. In fact I went to the pictures with Roy and regretted it very much. So the next time Richie asked I said "yes" straight away and we shared a double seat in the *Cach*. That used to be the local cinema, The Picturedrome, and everybody called it the *Cach* which means in Welsh excrement. I don't remember a thing about the film — I was trembling so much. And he didn't even touch me although we were sitting in a double seat designed for courting. But then Richie was never a toucher. Not one of your gropers. He had more class than that. In a strange way I became his "bird", but it was all very innocent.'

Richard went out with Catherine more than any other girl, and some people viewed them as a young couple with an idyllic relationship. Richard's younger brother was one. 'I was a year younger than Cathy,' he says, 'and at that time a year made all the difference. I used to dream of having something going like Richie. To me it was the biggest romance since Nelson Eddy and Jeanette MacDonald. I thought Cathy was the most beautiful girl in the world with that red hair and that shape and style. I was terribly jealous.'

Miss Dolan, as Catherine West, wife of an American novelist, laughs about it now. 'Graham may well remember it as a great love affair, but it was no such thing. There was never anything serious like there is today. Things that you see in films now would not even be mentioned between a boy and girl in the Port Talbot of those days. I know that Richie and I would dodge the school dental inspections on a Friday and always end up on the wooden pier where we read poetry to each other. I know I make it sound like something out of *Peg's Own Paper*, because I was a very emotional young woman and he was a very sexy young man. But this was just the way of the times, our

66

particular society. Richard would say, "My hands are cold" — and for gawd's sake I'd offer him my gloves. It wasn't me being frigid or anything. It was just that we both recognised that things could have become too hot. Richard was never a letcher. He was attracted by thoughts, feelings, ideas. And anyway, he was more attracted by rugby football than he was by me. I was sixteen and innocent and gormless about sex; and he liked me just for what I was.'

As his classmate 'Luther' Lewis puts it: 'Richie was a man among boys — a hell of a character. He was put in a class where we were all a year younger, but he was university material all right. No doubt about that. Brilliant. A normal person who had academic ability and the right potential would have to swot hard, but he could do it without seeming to do anything but drink and that.

'I initially became friendly with him because we played rugby together. I remember we were playing Llanelly Grammar School and I got really done up in the scrum by my opposite number in the front row. A big bugger was putting the boot in non-stop. I was taking a fair bit of hammer and then this character banged me in the belly when I was going up for the ball in the line-out. I was nearly sick. Richie picked me up and said: "Right Luther change places." Well, we went down and Richie yelled, "Okay boys, let's have some shove." And when we broke there was this poor sod stretched out unconscious. After that Richie looked after me.

'I remember another time he was telling us about the time he took a girl up the mountain. She was a bit of a goer and Richie had met her when he was in the Co-op. We were all standing around in the playground and waiting for him to come to the juicy part. Well. He used to suffer something chronic from boils, and he had this big one on his arse and the girl suddenly grabbed him right on it. And Richie let out such a yell that she ran hell for leather down the mountain and left him there. That was Richie all over. Always telling stories against himself. Never a show off, if you get me, and yet somehow he'd never let anyone get the better of him.'

Most boys came to regard him as their natural leader, but despite his cavalier style he was grimly aware that this unique second chance at school could end at any time. Acting, thanks to Leo, was the one career that attracted him, and Philip Burton was the one man with the means to help him. Deliberately and calculatingly he set out to impress and court the teacher and his first opportunity came with the school production of *Gallows Glorious*, a play about American abolitionist John Brown. Since the play had been partly cast the previous term there was only a small role available. Richie made certain he got the part of John Brown's brother Owen.

Dennis Burgess, who was Richard's best friend, says: 'Rich told me he was going to be an actor and that he was going to get Phil Burton to help him. That is why he did such a tremendous scene in *Gallows Glorious*. There is a terribly emotional thing at the end when Owen imagines he has seen the army of John Brown marching through the clouds. I am teaching drama now, and when you get boys of fifteen or sixteen to let themselves go — with tears, chokes in the voice and the rest — it is a remarkable thing. And Rich did it without being coaxed. He brought it out himself. And he was clever with it. He didn't do this at rehearsal, only on the night of the performance. I shall always remember Phil's face. He was in the wings and he couldn't believe it. He turned round to me and said, "Good God, that Jenkins. I'll kill him!" Afterwards he tore into him saying: "What do you think you were doing out there? Did you think that was good? You do realise you've probably ruined the play." And he went on talking about dramatic balance and how he had sweated blood over rehearsals to get the balance absolutely right. "Don't do it again, boy. Never again." But Richie did. Every night I asked him whether he was going to stop and he answered, "No, once I'm up on the stage there's nothing anyone can do."'

Brinley Jenkins, who was apparently outstanding in the main role of John Brown, told me: 'Richard didn't have much to do, but he always had this walk, this magnetism — the power to draw people's eyes. We did a lot of things later, but after that play Richard always took the lead. We were rivals. Phil Burton used to organise these competitions for speech and character in a Shakesperian role. When Richard first came back to school I used to win. I was probably the only boy who could beat him at anything because he was a brilliant student and captain of rugby and cricket. But then, after a month or so, he could even beat me at that. Yet he'd let me win the reading prize, because he always had this generosity, which was very rare in that type of competitive boy.'

Richard revealed his promise as an actor at an especially propitious time in the life of Philip Burton. His star pupil Flying Officer Tom Owen-Jones was no more — he had died of sarcoma, a rare cancerous condition, after damaging his hip in a parachute fall. Mr Burton was becoming more and more aware of this fascinating young creature, Richard Jenkins. He seemed to be always in his sightline. At the Youth

Centre, in A.T.C. training, during firewatching and at school. Phil Burton was intrigued. Meredith Jones was right.

'He didn't discover me,' Richard has since said. 'I discovered him.' And so, in a sense, he did.

Phil Burton's landlady, Mrs Elizabeth Smith, now dead, and her two daughters, Elizabeth and Audrey, remember Mr Burton coming into their house at 6 Connaught Street, which was a few terraced streets lower down from The Side, and saying that he had a pupil outside who had nowhere to spend the night because there had been trouble at home.

What trouble? Did Richard deliberately pick a quarrel with Elfed and walk out because he knew that there was a room vacant in Mrs Smith's house? Certainly Elfed could not afford to keep his wife's brother who was nearly seventeen and would be called up for service by the time he left school. As far as Elfed James was concerned, Richard was a dead loss.

Graham remembers the atmosphere between his brother and Elfed as being very strained. 'I remember when I stayed there that Elfed used to fall asleep on the sofa in the living room and Richard would look at him with contempt. In the end I reckon Richard just walked out.'

Did he intend going back to Hilda who now had Daddy Ni living with her in Pontrhydyfen? Or was he aware, as many pupils who are now schoolteachers in Taibach were, that Phil Burton had tried to adopt another boy that very year?

Whatever the reason, events moved at a pace that surprised even Richard. Mr Burton was virtually one of the Smith family because he had been with them for seventeen years — ever since he arrived in Taibach and they were living in Broad Street. But within a few months Richard became one of the family, too — with Phil Burton as his guardian. Whether Dic-bach-y-saer recognised the enormous advantages for his son or whether he had long lost the notion of responsibility in the haze of the Miner's arms is not known. Perhaps he agreed to the legal adoption because he knew full adoption was impossible. Phil Burton — born on 30 November 1904 — failed by twenty days to fulfil the legal requirement of being twenty-one years older than the boy he wished to adopt. Nevertheless Phil Burton had a legal document drawn up and executed to make Richard his ward, and at the same time Richard's surname was legally changed to avoid confusion, and probably to spare his cheerful but feckless father's feelings. He called himself Jenkins, however, until he left school.

Audrey Smith showing me Richard's room reflects, 'It is amazing to think how Philip Burton came home on a winter's night and asked mother if she would have a boy called Richard Jenkins to stay here as he had nowhere to go. Had she refused to have him, there may never have been a Richard Burton. Little did we know then what fate had in store for him. Richard came to stay the night and this became his home for the next two and a half years. This was his room and in the evenings he worked with Mr Burton in the room downstairs at the front. He was a nice boy, and the one thing I always admired was that he would never ask Mr Burton for anything. He was often very broke, but he was never a sponger. I remember how he would go down to the toilet at the bottom of the garden to smoke and drink. Mr Burton would come in and say, "Where's Richie?" And I used to say I didn't know and smoke would be pouring out of the door of the toilet.'

'Ma' Smith, still wonderfully alert at the age of ninety-five, when I met her, said: 'I glory in Richard's success. He has worked so very hard. You know Mr Burton would be up with him at all hours talking and studying. They would learn a play between them in a night. And sometimes they would wake me up and I would think they were quarrelling in the front room. Then I'd tap from the bed and I could hear them tiptoeing upstairs.

'When Richard came here from Caradoc Street he had nothing at all. Mr Burton bought him his clothes. He coached him, trained him, did everything. Richard has got to thank him for everything in the world he's got. He was a pretty rough boy then, and we had to polish him up a little. I taught him everything in manners — how to hold a knife and fork, how to eat his soup. But really he was the type of boy you couldn't alter. He had his own character and he was quite set in his ways even at that age. I remember once he stayed out all night after he and Mr Burton had a little bit of a fuss. He slammed out and said, "You'll see me when I get back." And oh! Mr Burton waited up half the night. I happened to be down early in the morning and there was Richard at the door looking bedraggled and very sorry for himself. "Where in the world have you been?" I asked. And he answered. "Sitting on my grandmother's grave all night. Meditating."

'Now that other boy who used to come here, Owen-Jones, he was very different: exceptionally handsome-looking, and definitely a gentler, more cultured type. Yet he also came from a mining family, and so did another boy Mr Burton helped. This was Viv Allen who has got on very well. He lives in a lovely house in London and he is headmaster of a school. But, oh, if you saw the miner's house he came from — a lean-to place with only a toilet at the bottom of the garden. And when you think of those lads, where they were born and where they were brought up, its extraordinary. Now Richie is entertaining in the Dorchester.

'He was a rougher type altogether when he first came here. Very outspoken.

'What came into his mind he would say, and he didn't care who he offended. Ask his opinion and you would get it. He had a wonderful memory. Yet he could be so forgetful about his clothes. Someone gave him a new mackintosh and he immediately lost it when he went down to the YMCA for a rehearsal. And, oh yes, I remember, he had such smelly feet. His socks! I used to say to Mr Burton, "Take those things out into the back yard." And even then you couldn't go near them for a couple of days. Oh, but Richard had so many good points. You had to like him. He was always in a rush, leaving it until the last minute to go to school. And I remember he used to like Shredded Wheat for breakfast, and Mr Burton was so spoiling him that he used to sprinkle sugar on for him.'

A boy enjoying such a close personal relationship with a master could have been bitterly resented by his school colleagues. Yet Richard never was. For one thing he never courted privilege. And secondly, while Burton worked wonders in improving his mind and speech, Richard's basic quality never changed; in school he was as strong-willed and unmanageable as he had been in his Caradoc Street days.

Luther Lewis remembers him coming to school 'when he was completely cut. He had been in the Grand Hotel all lunchtime and he reeked of beer. Burton was taking the class and he said to him,

"Richard, get home at once." Another time Richie belted a master who was knocking me about for something I hadn't done. He was reported to old Reynolds the headmaster, and any other boy would have been expelled. But somehow Richie got away with it. I think Phil Burton wanted to control him, but I don't think he ever got to first base.'

Dennis Burgess agrees with this assessment. 'Richard was working very hard with Phil Burton and there were a number of occasions when it was perfectly obvious that they hadn't come to school on the best of terms. There had been a row or something.

'At these times, when he might be remorseful, Phil Burton would be very amusing in class and have everyone laughing at his jokes. Everyone, that is, except Richard who would deliberately stay granite-faced. It was rather sad in a way, and these were the only occasions I felt like telling him to come off it. But mostly Richard's reactions were remarkable for his age. He had this extraordinary adult attitude, this maturity and almost worldly sophistication that set him apart from other boys. I was terrified of Phil Burton, and as for the headmaster, Mr Reynolds, he would have awed Frankenstein. But not Richie. There was a rule at the time that the main doors were to be used by staff, sixth formers and prefects. Richie always used the main doors and eventually he was caught. Reynolds called him up before the entire assembly at school, and he walked down the aisle and up to the stage as though he were about to receive the Oscar. Reynolds sarcastically went through the rules. "Are you a sixth former? Are you a prefect?" And so on. We quaked. Then, Reynolds said: "You're a big boy, Jenkins, aren't you?" The school waited in suspense. "If you say so, sir," said Richie. Another pause. "Well, in that case, Jenkins, I think I had better make you a prefect here and now."

'And he did. And for Reynolds this was completely out of character. Even in the ordinary way boys were never made prefects in front of the entire school. But Richie was. You see these things just happened to him all the time. Nothing was ever ordinary. As a schoolboy he was ten times larger than life and whatever happened to him was invariably dramatic. He had this, how can I say it, this cheerful disregard. For example, after playing rugby against Abertillery away, we were coming back in a non-corridor train when Richard desperately wanted a slash. Someone suggested that the only place was out of the window. The man was joking. But Richard threw up the window and pissed as we roared through a station with people lining the platform. And that was the first public appearance of Richard Burton in Wales.'

Burgess recalls another incident in the gym. 'For some reason Richie gave this master who used to take us for PT hell. The regular master had been called up for the Army and his replacement was not popular with the boys and probably Richie wanted to cut him down to size. The master never questioned Richard's extraordinary get-up for gym. Richie would take off his shirt but leave on his collar and tie, plus socks and suspenders and a tiny pair of shorts that he borrowed from the smallest boy in Form 11. This master didn't know what to do. The climax came when the master was bending over a large chest in which we kept all the sports gear. For some reason he got inside and as he was stooping Richie promptly closed the lid and sat on top of the box. The master was beating and hammering from the inside and making all kinds of terrible threats. But Richie just sat there. The rest of us were terrified and then I looked out of the window and saw Pop Reynolds approaching the gymnasium. "Watch out," I said. "Here comes the boss." We were now petrified, including the master. Richie knocked on the lid of the box and simply said. "Mr Reynolds is on his way over." Silence. "You do realise of course when the boss comes in I shall have to stand out of politeness." Still dead silence. It was like something out of an Abbot and Costello film. And when the headmaster entered, Richie made a great noise in getting off the box, but the lid didn't open. The headmaster looked around suspiciously, looked at Richard and said, "Have you seen the PT master?" The box loomed large and still. "Yes sir." "When?" "In the lesson, sir." The boss looked quizzically at Rich. "Why are you dressed like that?" "Changing, sir." "Those your shorts?" "No, sir. Borrowed them." "From a midget?" "No, sir." The boss looked at our tight-lipped expressions and walked out. How much he guessed I don't know.

'Anyway, Rich lifted the lid and said. "You can come out now." It was a joke and we laughed about it tremendously. But when it was all over Richard said to me, "What do you think of that then?" I told him I really didn't know what else the master could do and that I would have probably done the same. "Ah," said Richard. "But you wouldn't have got yourself into that situation in the first place. That's the difference. For a person to allow himself to get into such a position with boys like us! The lack of dignity!"

'It all seems a childish prank now, but the point is that no other boy thought of it the way he did. To us it was just a hell of a good joke. But he saw the implications. He had this incredible maturity and awareness. He used to say, "What is it? Is it something we've got? Or is it something they lack?" Profound. I have met Richard many times since our schooldays and looking back there is so much of his character that shows in the little things that happened then. His reactions were never the sort you would expect from an ordinary schoolboy.'

Despite all the time he gave to sport, acting and girls. Richard did not waste his second chance at school. In September, 1943, he had two mentions in the *Port Talbot Guardian*. The local critic praised Phil Burton's production of *Pygmalion* and hailed Richard's portrayal of Professor Higgins as a triumph. 'He displayed a dramatic talent that made him a dominating personality and brought out all that was best in the acting of his opposite number, Dilys Jones, as the London flower girl.' Elsewhere in the paper the results of the Central Welsh Board school examinations were published. Richard got 'very goods' in English Literature and Maths, 'credits' in English language, history, Welsh and (surprisingly) chemistry with a 'pass' in geography.

Then at summer camp with the 499 Squadron, Flight-Lieutenant Philip Burton read an advertisement in the *Western Mail*, 'Emlyn Williams wants young Welsh actors for small parts in a new play which will open in the autumn.' His Flight-Sergeant, Richard Burton, successfully applied.

Chapter Six

PROBABLY THE GREATEST monument to those extraordinary and dedicated teachers who shaped rough Welsh schoolboys and made them aware of a world outside the cages of coal was built by Stanley Baker in a palatial, eleventh-floor executive suite with a wide-screen view of the Thames stretching from the Houses of Parliament to the Tower of London. There he sat with large cigar — a movie tycoon, television producer and film star. More than anyone else he knew Burton *when* ... when they were both young and raw and stepping onto the professional stage for the first time ... when, simply because of the geography, they thought being the sons of coalminers was commonplace and that all other accents were affected and belonged to a minority who strived to ape their betters.

Stanley, who died long before he should from cancer and was knighted for his services to the arts, looked out of the window towards the West End and pointed. 'When Richard and I were over there at St Martin's theatre I don't think either of us could claim burning ambitions to stay on as actors. I certainly couldn't. One's main ambition from the earliest sort of remembrances was to get out of the valleys. It didn't matter which way — through football, boxing anything so long as you left the valleys and improved yourself. There was no passionate desire to be an actor, great or bad. It was simply an opportunity provided at the right time. It was an opportunity to go to London at an early age and earn money. I used always to think as a kid that Cardiff was England — and yet it was only twenty miles away. That's how far withdrawn we were. We just had to grab the chance to widen our horizons.

'I didn't know who Emlyn Williams was. I knew he was the boss, that he had written and directed the play and that he came from North Wales. But there was a sense of unreality about the whole bloody thing — to be suddenly taken out of a Welsh valley and thrust into big cities, totally alone. When I think about it now, I would never have let my son go off under those circumstances at the age of fourteen. Maybe that attitude is too protective, maybe I'm getting softer. But it never occurred to my parents. All that concerned them was that I was earning a fiver a week.

'It was a bit different of course with Richard. He was eighteen. He should have been in the army. Emlyn must have got him a deferment. He had a much better education than I had. He'd been to secondary school, of course, which made all the difference as I was telling you. He knew all about Emlyn but little did he think that this man who, let's face it was instrumental in getting him into the theatre, would later launch him on his film career and introduce him to his wife Sybil. But at that time he didn't have that much to do, I was his understudy and had less to occupy my time. The play was called *The Druid's Rest* and he played the small role of the elder brother of a rather imaginative boy who is always suspecting strangers in this eccentric Welsh pub. I best remember the theatre next door. It was a revue with Hermione Gingold, and the chorus girls used to sunbathe on the roof of the Ambassadors right below us. Richard and I — shows how daft we were — used to aim pea shooters at them trying to hit their tits. We lived in digs in Gower Street and the things we got up to are incredible when you look back. We were like wild animals let loose to enjoy the birds and the booze; two Welsh kids, totally disorientated, absolutely free of any sort of control at all. In these days if a kid comes into the theatre, there are all sorts of laws and regulations; they have chaperones and all that sort of bollocks. We had none of that. I looked much older than my years, and at eighteen, come to think of it, Richard wouldn't be trusted with one.

'So we drank ourselves stupid. Really we did, and Richard could pull any bird he chose. He had the gift and the looks and the gab. But whatever we are today we can thank those amazing schoolteachers. Its odd isn't it. The three of us. Emlyn, Richard and myself would not have people like yourself showing curiosity if it hadn't been for them. You know my fellow, that dear marvellous man Glyn Morse, had put me ahead of Richard at that time. Somehow or other he persuaded the film producer Sergei Nolbandov to watch me in a school play in the Rhondda and I got a small part in his movie *Undercover*.

'Morse had a family of his own, and yet he gave me private elocution lessons, took me to London for my first film part and, like Phil Burton did with Richard, got me into my first play.

'After I left Wales he sent me one book every week and I had to read it and every Sunday, no matter what, I had to write at least eight pages about it. Then he got me into Birmingham Rep and though I was working

81

very hard there, he used to send me two books each week to read and discuss. This went on until I was about twenty-five years of age, and after I became successful. In a strange way he guided my career. I don't know what it was. Some strange kind of instinct about what one should do, what moves one should make next. He is retired now and half blind, but to this day I will take his advice.

'Until I was twelve I was totally hopeless at school. Got into awful trouble. Then I met Morse, the arts and crafts master, and for the first time in my life I wanted to go to school. I didn't do ordinary lessons like arithmetic, English and science. I just went to his class every morning and stayed there all day long.'

There were only seven others in the entire cast: Michael Shepley as the mysterious wayfarer, Roddy Hughes as the innkeeper, Gladys Henson as his wife, Neil Porter, a Welsh bard, Lyn Evans, Nuna Davies and the young boy Brynmor Thomas.

Miss Henson, who played Richard's stage mother, remembers the first time she met him at rehearsals. 'He was the most beautiful looking boy I'd ever seen. He was lovely. And he seemed so calm and collected. I thought perhaps he would be nervous, but not a bit of it. You would never have thought it was his first professional part. He was really a natural from the word go, from that first rehearsal almost. He was always lolling about, always so calm. He took everything in his stride. He may have been more excited than he pretended to be. I don't know. But certainly the theatre was quite secondary to his interest in rugby; he never stopped talking about the game.

'I remember one day he was lying on the sofa at rehearsals, dozing off, and I said to him, "Oh Richard, you're never going to be an actor if you go on like this. You must keep your place. Don't go to sleep in the middle of rehearsals." And he said, "Oh you know me, Glad, I go my own way." Yet he was never a precocious boy; just an ordinary boy with great talent.'

The first night was 26 January 1944, and next morning the reviews were hard to find. The newspapers were restricted in size and much of the space was given to the struggle for Leningrad and the battle of Cassino. There were two mentions of Burton. *The Times* critic wrote: 'Mr Richard Burton (or should it be Master Richard?) is consistently droll as the small boy whose starved imagination spins the web of misunderstandings.' The critique was also a web of misunderstanding. The man from *The Times* had obviously identified Richard with the part played by Brynmor Thomas. Later the *New Statesman* concluded its review with the line 'In a wretched part Richard Burton showed exceptional ability.'

It was a modest debut. But Emlyn Williams was impressed and agreed with Joshua Logan, the American director and dramatist, who happened to be in the audience and predicted a great future for Burton. 'Richard was obviously going to be a great actor,' says Emlyn. 'He had the looks, the ease, the deportment and the natural flair. But you couldn't foresee his future precisely because he had only the one small comedy scene which he played with tremendous assurance, as if he had been in the theatre for years. It is a paradox in a way that he never became a great comedian rather than a serious actor because it was the comedy scene that persuaded me that the potential was there and that he had tremendous reserves of natural timing.'

When Burton was working in London the worst days of the blitz had passed and the allies dominated the air as the second front was launched. The war was being won. The West End's square mile of theatres and pubs was the most exciting place on earth. During one scene in the play Richard and his stage mother had to go upstairs, ostensibly to get ready for church. 'Every night we went up to a kind of landing,' says Miss Henson. 'We always had about a quarter of an hour wait together, and while we were up there Richard used to tell me about his love life. "Oo! I met the most lovely nurse last night, Glad," he would say. And I should think he did have a love life because he was gorgeous to look at.'

Little did he know that twenty years later his love life with an actress, who was reminding the GIs of their sisters back home, would make world headlines. He had no time for movies, and even if he had, it is doubtful whether he would have ventured into the Empire, Leicester Square where an eleven-year-old girl called Elizabeth Taylor was stealing a film from a dog in *Lassie Come Home*.

After the curtain Richard liked nothing better than to join the cast at the Two Brewers pub just around the corner and persuade the chorus girl from the Ambassadors that he had something far more interesting than the pea shooter that he and Stanley had teased them with. And it was here that he was given a farewell party.

Six months later, in the autumn of 1944, Nevill Coghill, Merton Professor of English Literature and Sub-Rector of Exeter College, was updating the college undergraduate card index file, noting examinations passed and trying to make some perceptive comment on each student. The difficulty was to assess those students received from the Armed Forces for the special wartime University Short Course; but when Coghill came to the name of an eighteen-year-old RAF cadet from Wales he wrote unhesitatingly: 'This boy is a genius and will be a great actor. He is outstandingly handsome and robust, very masculine and with deep inward fire, and extremely reserved.'

This, after six months' acquaintance, was the learned don's opinion of Richard Burton of Taibach. And time has not tempered his judgment. He told me: 'I have had many students of very great gifts and many of very little. But I have had only two men of genius to teach — W.H. Auden and Richard Burton. When they happen one cannot mistake them.'

Genius. An extraordinary word to describe the son of a miner and a barmaid who was to leave Oxford as he had arrived: without any academic distinction whatsoever and to end his war service, not as a combat pilot, as intended, but as a humble Aircraftsman Second Class.

Yet, Robert Hardy, the Shakesperean and popular TV actor, who was in the same squadron as Richard at Oxford, chooses the same noun to describe him. 'He was a genius in the effortless way he attracted everybody — the most attractive creature I have ever come across, in the true sense of that adjective. It was the size of his personality that made me think of him as a great man.

'Everything about him was larger than life. But not in an actorish way. He did not give the impression of an actor throwing it on. He was a fine athlete, brilliant talker, superb drinker, everything. He was a sort of Renaissance man. We read things like Castiglione's *The Courtier* — sixteenth century instructions on how to be a perfect man — and it seemed to us at Oxford that this was just the sort of man he was. A natural born prince.'

At first any reputation he had at Oxford rested entirely on his prodigious drinking capacity. 'Beer Burton' they called him, and he laid claim to the Exeter sconce record — part of a dining hall punishment for bad etiquette in which the offender must drink nearly two pints of beer in thirty seconds or pay for it. According to Richard he learned to drink without swallowing and could sink a sconce in ten seconds. Drinking records were the only sporting honours open to him at Oxford. But he was resolved at least to widen his acting experience in the short time he was there. In the summer of 1944, Oxford's famous but bankrupt University Dramatic Society was midway through its decade of suspension, and a substitute company called 'The Friends of the OUDS' was staging a series of productions to pay off the society's debts. The moving spirit behind 'The Friends', and destined to become the father-figure of the Oxford Theatre, was Professor Coghill. Richard tackled him with the same single-mindedness he displayed when approaching Philip Burton for a part.

'What do you want?' said Coghill when the young Welshman knocked at his study door.

'I have come to recite some poetry to you,' Richard replied.

'Well, there's a dais over there. Stand on it, and say it.'

Richard recited the soliloquy. 'To be or not to be ...' And Coghill was impressed. 'Well you need no help from me. That was perfect. But what do you want?'

'I would like a part in *Measure for Measure*.'

'I'm afraid it's fully cast. But there's likely to be a

86

vacancy for the part of Angelo. If you care to understudy for it, you can have it. Maybe the vacancy will occur.'

Richard moved towards the door. 'Thank you then. I will.'

'Hey, what's your name, by the bye?' the Professor called out.

'Richard Burton.'

Coghill explained to me: 'I do not often recall conversations verbatim, but this one impressed itself on me. I can still hear the melodious Welsh voice and way of speaking which was at once changed for received standard English when he started "To be or not to be". The change was utterly convincing and instantaneous. Out came the most perfect rendering I have ever heard except that given a short while before by John Gielgud in his Haymarket *Hamlet*. But it was not just an imitation of Gielgud.'

Richard tells a dramatic yarn of how he moved from understudying to playing Angelo. 'The chap playing the part was so impressed by my earnestness that he said I should play half the performances and he would play the other half. Then he became ill and vanished.'

Professor Coghill remembers it differently. 'The chap was the late Hallham Fordham, who had won distinction for his BBC reading of Wordsworth's *The Prelude*. At the time he was an RAF officer and he had already played Oberon and Horatio for me. He warned me that he expected shortly to be posted elsewhere, and I was on tenderhooks for fear that he would be taken from me, until Richard appeared and my king was guarded by an ace. In due course Hallham was posted away and Richard stepped effortlessly into the part.'

Coghill was so impressed with Burton's Angelo that

87

he invited Hugh Beaumont, the suave Welsh managing director of H.M. Tennent to come down and see him act. Tennent's was the major producing company, responsible for presenting *The Druid's Rest* and Beaumont, once assistant manager of the Cardiff Playhouse and nicknamed Binkie (in Welsh, darkie) since his childhood days, was fast on the way to becoming the most powerful theatre manager in London. After the performance he told Richard to call as soon as he had finished his service in the RAF.

Not everyone thought so highly of Richard's performance. A student critic wrote: Mr Burton is pretty, with a good voice and nothing else.' But Coghill dismissed the critique. 'No, no,' he told me. 'Student critics are notable for their cattiness and bitchiness, and have an art to combine what is foul in both cat and dog. Moreover, they have little experience or judgment, and are more interested in drawing attention to their own personalities than to the subject of their journalising. There was nothing "pretty" either in face or manner about Richard; he was simply the most manly-handsome boy I can remember and, from the start, acted with distinction and strength. Richard's *stillness* was overwhelming while he was being unmasked in the last act by the Duke. He stood absolutely erect, facing the audience with all the anguish in the world in his eyes, and with his arms at his side, his fingers clenched, yet ever so slightly unclenching and clenching again — an almost invisible, yet overwhelming movement; his features motionless like stone. I think I may have told him this gesture, but he did it so much more grandly (if that is the right word for something almost imperceptible) than I had expected. It was one of those manifestations that made me know his greatness as an actor. You couldn't not look at him. You couldn't not feel with him'.

When Richard left Oxford he was one of twelve prize-winning cadets in the passing out parade of the University Air Squadron. Another was a Jewish boy called Mick Misell who had been born over a fish and chip shop in East London and was now studying to become a scientist. Misell didn't like Burton the first time they met. 'I can't think why we were among the prize cadets. Perhaps because he was an actor and I was something of an athlete. Anyway we sat at the same table in the mess and he started to have a dig at the number of Jews who controlled the West End theatre. I said, "Hey, come off it, we're fighting a war against that sort of thing." And then we had a terrible stand-up argument and I accused him of being highly anti-semitic and a black shirt bastard.'

Burton stepped down and they shook hands. The Welshman and the Jew became firm friends during the next three years they were stationed together. They trained in Canada as Pilot-navigator-bomb-aimers but the only fighting they experienced was in bars. 'I remember him coming back one night with his face smashed to pieces,' says Misell. 'We passed out in pubs, but we never passed out as officers. We were due to get our wings when the whole bloody thing was called off. It was VJ Day. We were flown back to Bercham Newton in Norfolk and we were just left alone by the brass. We lived an unbelievable life of absolute autonomy — reading, fucking and poaching. It was a complete skive and it was through Richie I threw up all idea of becoming a scientist and going back to Oxford. He formed a Welsh Male Choir — even though he was the only Welshman there. I can still remember the harmonies now, and at that time I admired him so much that I was very keen on becoming naturalised Welsh. I felt that if you were Welsh and Jewish you couldn't miss.

'It was thanks to Richie that I first took up acting — and I played Richard Burton because, as usual he had got himself involved with too many women. You see he had met this girl, only once very briefly in the dark, and had given her the chat. He never wasted time. So it was a cert, but he forgot about this other darling. So he rang her up and said, "By the way. You've got no racial prejudice, because I'm Jewish." So posing as Burton I went to meet this lovely girl. She was a hairdresser: very sexy, and she had money. And when she first met me, she remarked, "You're very tiny to be skipper of the station rugby side." And I said, "Well, you don't have to be big, girl. It's how you hit 'em that counts." You know I actually learned my first lines of Shakespeare to play that role. She knew he had been an actor so I learned, parrot fashion from Rich — "Tis now the very witching time of night." I quoted it to her down by the river bank in King's Lynn and as we walked around the town the lads would say "Hello Mick." She asked what they had said, I told her "They said Dick, Dick." I kept this up for about three weeks, and all the time she really thought I was Richard Burton the actor.'

Richard Burton's stand-in really became an actor. Mick Misell changed his name by deed poll to Warren Mitchell, and as Alf Garnett, the foul-mouthed bigot of *Till Death Us Do Part,* became Britain's best known television character.

While Mick was impersonating Dick, Richard became involved with one very special girl whom he could only see at weekends by making marathon journeys by train, and no sooner were they together than it seemed to be time to make the journey back to the station. The girl was an actress, Eleanor

Summerfield. He had met her in London when he had special leave to play in a BBC television production of *The Corn Is Green*.

Richard called her 'Boots' (a nickname is even now an indication of serious intent) and wrote to her regularly (another indication of interest). They became unofficially engaged. 'I thought he was absolutely marvellous,' Miss Summerfield told me. 'I had never met anyone with quite his sort of application of words, and I thought there was no reason why he shouldn't become the greatest actor in the world. He had all the kind of Welsh passion for the theatre, which was fantastically invigorating. He used to see me every weekend he could get off and sometimes I'd be playing the provinces.'

In April 1947 they managed to have five days together. She was touring with the play *Dr Jekyll and Mr Hyde* and Richard joined her in Scotland and shared digs with Donald Huston, a Welsh actor who had completed his RAF service. Donald was then agonisingly in love with actress Brenda Hogan who, he recalls, 'didn't want to know'. But ironically he eventually wooed and won Miss Hogan while Richard and Eleanor went their separate ways. 'I honestly can't remember why we decided not to go on with it,' said Miss Summerfield. 'Our temperaments didn't fit or something — anyway we decided that this was not going to work.'

A performance that Misell much admires took place as they came to the end of their three years' National Service. Richard, who had studied mediaeval Italian at Oxford, was called into a court-martial as an interpreter to help defend an Italian prisoner-of-war accused of raping a land girl. He discovered, to his horror, that the defendant spoke an obscure dialect which he couldn't understand. But he recognised the plaintiff as none other than 'Doking Lil', a local roll-in-the-hay whose character he understood all too well.

But Richard, having found his stage, wasn't going to fluff his lines or bow out for anyone. He looked at Lil, in her boy scout hat and sturdy riding breeches, and then at the sad faced Italian in patched uniform, and could only conclude that she had raped him. So, as the Italian swore to the Blessed Virgin or whatever in unintelligible ice-cream, Richard based his hazardous translation on the simple premise that all Italians looked the same to Lil and this was clearly a case of mistaken identity. The man was acquitted. Richard's one achievement in all those farcical time-wasting years was his perverse delight in having been of service to the enemy.

A few months after they had been demobbed in November 1947, Burton and Misell happened to meet in Shaftesbury Avenue. 'Well,' said Richard, 'What are you planning to do in civvy street?'

'I'm going to the Royal Academy of Dramatic Art.'

'Good God!' Burton exclaimed. 'Don't tell me you're going to become a bloody actor.'

'That's right. And what are you doing?'

'Bloody marvellous. I've got a contract with Tennent's. Five hundred quid a year! Guaranteed ten pounds a week whether I work or not.'

Warren Mitchell recalls their conversation with a wry grin. 'It was really funny because a few months later I went backstage to see Richie who was appearing in his first West End showpiece and I congratulated him on doing so well. "Like hell I am Mick. Like hell I am!" he said 'Do you know what the mean bastards are paying me? Just ten quid a week!'

Chapter Seven

WHEN EX-AIRCRAFTSMAN Richard Burton strolled back into the theatre with a Tennent's contract in his pocket the roles offered were tiny and of little consequence, but his impact was immediate and lasting; not on the critics nor the public but on his peers who were captivated by his natural aristocratic arrogance, his imperial contempt for authority and his instinctive generosity to the ambition of those who were straining on tiptoe and aspiring towards goals beyond their grasp. Today, those selfsame actors, who have nothing to gain by brushing his present fame, are as lavish in their assessment of his potential genius as they obviously were when he arrived for rehearsals for *Castle Anna* at the Lyric Theatre, Hammersmith.

He had been given the small part of a gentleman officer, but was also understudying the leading man who had been summoned before a Conscientious Objectors' tribunal and was in danger of being removed from the part. On the day of the hearing the director Daphne Rye — she had first auditioned him for *The Druid's Rest* and was much taken with him — called a full rehearsal to see what kind of cover she had in a young man she hadn't seen for four years.

Actress Pauline Letts recalls: 'It was the morning

after the opening night and everyone was feeling a little unhappy. Then something electric happened. He was quite brilliant in the part. Since then, over the years, I have worked with many actors and actresses who went on to become very big stars, but he was the only one whom one knew absolutely from the beginning was destined for greatness.

'I can only tell you the feeling I had about him — the impact of this tremendous brain and talent. During that day we sat around talking and became very deep about personalities and the pyschological aspects of life, and I remember very well him saying that he had a sort of other-half sitting on his shoulder and watching everything he did all the time, and that never under any circumstances was he non-objective. This objective self was watching everything he did. Most good actors do this, but he had developed it very early. It was there then. And I remember everybody's dilemma because they would have liked him in the leading part, but at the same time they were very fond of the leading man and didn't want him to go to jug.'

The leading man didn't go to jug, and Richard didn't get his part. Another actor, who became disenchanted with Burton for personal reasons outside the theatre, has since said that he was amazed by Richard's indifference to what any other young actor in the sticks would have regarded as the magnifying glass of fame. He was with him in another Tennent play, *Dark Summer* which was touring the provinces, when Burton shot off to London for the day. He didn't tell anyone where he was going and that night backstage he was handed a telegram. It read: YOU HAVE WON THE SCHOLARSHIP. When the actor asked him what it meant Burton replied: 'I've got the sort of juvenile lead in a film that

Emlyn Williams is making called *The Last Days of Dolwyn*.'

Then he crumpled up the cable, drop-kicked it into the night and was more concerned about getting to the pub before it closed than wasting time in crowing to the rest of the cast. 'Do you know,' said the actor. 'He didn't even bother to reply.'

Such nonchalance is difficult to believe, yet Emlyn Williams confirms Richard's amazing insouciance. 'I remember saying when he turned up for his first day's work on the set, "Oh, it's you. We were just about to replace you because we thought you hadn't accepted the part". He was, and still is, hopelessly unbusinesslike when it comes to acknowledging contracts and hurtfully casual in conducting relationships from afar. But women smiled at what they saw as the aberrations of a boy.

Recalling the first time he was with a woman, Richard characteristically tells a story — like the girl on the mountainside who clutched his boil — angled against himself but nevertheless revealing. It happened when he and a girl were in a half-bombed house in Liverpool. They lit a fire in the grate to keep warm. 'Eventually I fell asleep in front of the fire and my feet were right up against the flames and in time my boots became terribly hot. Well, I had this terrifying dream that my lost soul was being consumed by hell-fire, and because I had this strict chapel upbringing and had learned all about the wages of sin, you can imagine what an alarming experience it was.'

Not that it deterred Richard. 'Having discovered sex,' as he later expressed it, 'I began looting and plundering with great delight.' He saw the sex urge as the sweetness of life and the origin of all affections and the root of all aspirations.

One lunchtime at the London Film Studios, Isleworth, when the cast of *Dolwyn* were lazing outside in the summer sunshine, Emlyn asked: 'What did you do last night, Richard?'

'A floosie, a bootiful floosie. I took her to a nightclub and then ...'

Emlyn frowned. 'Really, you know it's time you settled down. Why don't you take out one of these nice girls who are in the picture. That one for instance. 'And he pointed to a slim, young girl sitting on the grass nearby. 'Now she's a real sweet girl. Her name is Williams, too. Sybil Williams.'

Richard laughed. 'Yes, all right. Why not? I'll introduce myself.' And he did, there and then.

Sybil Williams was an eighteen-year-old drama student, also in her first film, but only just. After the auditions Emlyn Williams had eliminated her from his short list because of her inability to speak fluent Welsh and a tight budget that restricted him to six girl extras. But he had relented when her professor of music telephoned, begging him to reconsider because the girl was so hard-working and desperately keen.

Emlyn says: 'I thought — oh to hell with it. Korda can afford it, for heaven's sake. Another eight quid a week won't hurt.'

After shooting a love scene with Andrea Lea, he tried to date her. She was interested but explained that she was taking her gold medal test at the drama academy. Richard took her telephone number and said he would ring her next day to hear how she had fared.

Sybil won her gold medal. And back at her flat she waited eagerly for his call. She waited until after midnight, but the phone remained silent.

Next morning she resolved to cut him dead on the

In the middle of *le scandale*, Richard and his first wife meet their 4-year-old daughter, Kate, at Rome airport. Exactly a year later, Sybil flew out of Burton's life POPPERFOTO

A new face – Burton arrives in Hollywood in 1953 with a three-film contract for *My Cousin Rachel, The Desert Rats* and *The Robe*
AQUARIUS

Above: Look Back in Anger, 1959. Young Burton blows his own trumpet as Jimmy   *ASSOCIATED BRITISH PICTURE CORP*

Below: As Antony in 1962. The start of a daring courtship and a public submission   *AQUARIUS*

Above: Richard playing the saint to Peter O'Toole's king in *Becket*, 1964 *AQUARIUS*

Below: The whisky-sodden ex-priest in *The Night of the Iguana*, 1964. Off-screen, Sybil became the ex-Mrs Burton *AQUARIUS*

Above: Genevieve Bujold rehearsing *Anne of The Thousand Days* in 1970. She won Hollywood's Golden Globe Award and said: 'I owe it all to Richard'   *LONDON EXPRESS NEWS SERVICE*

Below: Llareggub – the backward spelling of Dylan Thomas's village in *Under Milkwood*, made in 1971. It made sweet llareggub at the box-office

After the pressure of playing George and Martha in *Who's Afraid of Virginia Woolf?*, Richard and Elizabeth became co-producers as Petruchio and Katharina in *The Taming of the Shrew*, 1967

Many critics point to Alec Leamas as Burton's best performance as the seedy, shiftless secret agent he played in *The Spy Who Came in From The Cold*, 1965

Above: Chatting to Princess Margaret at the opening of *The Taming of the Shrew,* with Michael Redgrave *AQUARIUS*

Below: Elizabeth celebrates her 50th birthday and separation from her seventh husband. Richard flew in for the party *POPPERFOTO*

set. She wrote him off as another philandering, self-centred actor and that all the gossip she had heard about him was true.

But the moment they met she was knocked off balance. 'What the hell's the matter with your phone? I tried again and again to get through to you. But nothing. Bloody nothing.' Sybil was too wise to the devious ways of the Welsh to swallow that story, but was entirely seduced by his charm and interest. 'If you want to take me out to the theatre tomorrow night, telephone me tonight.' When she got home the telephone was ringing and thereafter they were inseparable.

Coincidentally, at that time, Burton and Stanley Baker were sharing a Thames houseboat at Chiswick with a couple of girl students who were suddenly given the cold shoulder. 'He just kept eulogising about this wonderful Welsh girl he had met at the studios,' said Baker. 'I didn't take much interest at the time, after all I reckoned there must be about a hundred thousand girls in Wales called Sybil Williams. But about two days later I met this Sybil. And it was incredible. I had gone to school with her in Ferndale. She was the daughter of the local under-manager of the pit, and I used to go around with her as a kid. Richard had never before spoken with such genuine enthusiasm about a girl before. He had named her. And that meant he wasn't using her. He never named names. Never boasted on conquests. But Sybil was different and Richard was right in his choice. She was a marvellous girl, the most attractive in the village, the most mature, the most interesting, the most friendly. Richard was absolutely dotty about her. She was like a kid sister to me and like anyone else from a mining village you are protective towards family, insanely so.

Sybil knew this, of course she did. And in my absolute delight in their friendship she was certain of his love. Talk about a perfect match! Well, it was quite incredible. They had everything in common. Not only background but in the way that circumstances had shaped them.

'Like Richard, Sybil had lost her mother as a child and was brought up by an older sister. And she too, had to leave school and work as a draper's assistant when her father died. Not only that but she made her mark in amateur dramatics and left the village when she was seventeen to make her mark in London.'

Sybil had no real acting opportunity in *The Last Days of Dolwyn*, but she was thrilled as a young actress just to be involved in a movie that had been nothing but an idle thought in the mind of a brilliant Welshman. Emlyn had told her that when Korda had asked him to write and direct a picture he didn't have an idea, until one day while bumping about the Welsh countryside in a bus he heard the driver call out: 'Over there is the reservoir. They couldn't make it you know without flooding the valley. Everybody was evacuated and the village had to go under.' It inspired Williams to write a scenario of a doomed Welsh village and an old lady's fight for its survival against a villainous land agent.

The dramatic ending was played out on location in Rhydymain, an enchanted village. Here Burton, as the young hero, had to struggle to the death with Emlyn Williams who becomes soaked in paraffin, rolls in the embers of a fire, goes up in flames and dies of shock. Then the old lady, Dame Edith Evans, had to save her foster son from a murder charge by climbing the great dam above the village and letting loose the mighty flood to engulf her beloved *Dolwyn* and cover her hated land agent.

Richard had seen Sybil almost every day of that long, idyllic summer of '48 and with the separating of ways he became acutely aware of how vital and important a part of his life she had become. He proposed and showed her off to the family at Cwmavon and Pontrhydyfen. They were all agreed — brothers, sisters, Daddy Ni — Syb was perfect. But it was difficult for them to make wedding plans. He was committed to radio work and a modest role in the film *Now Barabbas Was A Robber*; she was an assistant stage manager and understudy in *Harvey* starring Sid Field as a man whose best friend is a rabbit. They settled for a Kensington Registry Office ceremony.

The date was unfortunate — 5 February 1949. As it was a Saturday she was required on stage for a matinee that afternoon, and more horrifying from Richard's fanatical point of view, the date clashed with the Scotland–Wales rugby international at Murrayfield. Daphne Rye threw the reception in her home at 24 Pelham Crescent and after the bride and Sid Field left for the theatre, Richard and his muckers went upstairs and settled down with the remaining champagne to listen to the rugby commentary. Upstairs was another wedding present from the generous Daphne — a fully furnished small flat at a ridiculously low rental.

It was here Sybil found him when she returned from the theatre — sprawled among the dead men. The Scots had conquered by six points to five. She made him coffee and returned to the theatre. She would always put his interests before her own. Sybil was, in Richard's word, 'impeccable'.

Then, entirely out of the blue, came a shattering blow to his ego. After three days of rehearsals for

Terence Rattigan's *Adventure Story* he was fired and replaced by Robert Flemyng. 'I felt suicidal,' says Richard. 'Everybody had told me: "This is your big chance".' The play was about Alexander the Great and he had been given the role of Hephaeestion. It was a minor, but important part and it gave him the opportunity to measure up to Paul Scofield, three years his senior and the critic's darling after a tremendous two seasons of Shakespeare at Stratford.

Richard was so confident of the impact he would make in the West End that he shared his good fortune with Stanley Baker by helping him to get a walk-on part. Director Peter Grenville thought Burton too young to play Scofield's senior, and too short. Baker says that this explanation was 'a load of bullshit. Richie admired Scofield but he had this own overwhelming belief in his own personality. He came on too strong for the character he was playing.' Noel Willman, who was playing Darius, takes the same view. 'Richard was sacked simply because he was far too interesting. In his part he was meant to be a shadowy figure and Richard was never going to be a shadow no matter how hard he might try and he was jolly well not going to try. I don't mean he was being naughty about it. He was simply a star personality who was riveting, and to play a shadowy kind of figure behind Alexander just wasn't on.'

A star personality, maybe. But certainly not a star. At that time Burton was completely unknown to the public and was conscious of the tiny magic circle that controlled and made up the English theatrical scene. His success was more praised than recognised and his one failure seemed to be exaggerated out of all proportion to his standing. Just when he thought he had found the key to success he had discovered the wrong lock.

Robert Hardy, who had gone back to Oxford and had become a contemporary of another Welshman, Frank Hauser, the BBC drama producer, was concerned at the way in which his old RAF pal, Richard, was waving his key about in public places, particularly bars. He arranged a dinner between Hauser and Richard to discuss the possibility of Burton as Henry V in a radio production.

It was a stormy meeting. Richard arrived with a few on board and was fiercely aggressive and drunkardly arrogant. After threatening to throw Hauser through the window for daring to tell him how to play Henry, he reluctantly agreed to audition for the part.

Unbelievably, Richard was well in liquor when he turned up for the trial reading at Broadcasting House. 'He was still resentful at being sacked from a play that was obviously going to be a huge success,' says Hauser. 'And I think he had deliberately not studied the text. He did a good reading, though nothing like so good as he could have done. But something of the personality came across, and Archie Harding who was my boss, said "Okay, why not? If you are keen on using him, use him. It might be interesting." So we did the production and he was very good. Very honest, and very hardworking. I thought he was more successful in the quiet bits, but then on radio it's almost impossible to be successful in the loud bits of Shakespeare.'

It was well received and gave him confidence. But before he could start to strut, his pride was quickly deflated by a ghost from the past.

'Do you want me to be forthright about Henry?' asked Meredith Jones.

'Of course.'

Mered prodded him in the chest. 'My boy,' he roared. 'You were a weak, pale, piping, pusillanimous imitation of Laurence Olivier.'

John Gielgud didn't think so. As the director and leading man in a new Christopher Fry play *The Lady's Not For Burning* he was surprised by the casual arrogance of the young man playing the apprentice. Richard would loll around the stage talking passionately about everything, particularly rugby, and not seeming to show any interest in the play.

'I would become angry with him because he always began to yawn prodigiously when one o'clock lunchtime arrived,' says Sir John.

'I had heard about him. Beaumont rang me one day and said, "We've got this wonderful boy Richard Burton." And I said, "Oh really," rather unimpressed. And then he came to the first rehearsal and, of course, I was absolutely bowled over by his immediate understanding. He was perfect looking for the part. He spoke it beautifully. And in the second act we had a great, rather long, poetic scene between Pamela Brown and myself, while he played the boy scrubbing the floor. I always remember this. It was very difficult to do — with the boy stopping at intervals to come into the scene with a line or two. And when he had these lines to speak, he knew exactly what to do without my telling him. I didn't direct him at all in that play. He played the love scenes with the little girl and this scrubbing-the-floor sequence — in which he came into the scene and then retired from it — in the most wonderful way. Absolutely, you knew instinctively, even if you had your back to him, that he was feeding the scene exactly right.'

It was a scene that went unnoticed by the critics, yet

it seemed to have impressed the whole profession. Alec Guinness says, 'You could not miss him, because of his marvellous head and shoulders.'

Guinness became a friend of Sybil and Richard during the long run and so did Paul Scofield. Ironically, *The Lady's Not For Burning* was a far bigger success than *Adventure Story* and attracted a procession of celebrities to the Globe Theatre. The 'little girl' who Gielgud mentioned was a charming eighteen-year-old called Claire Bloom.

While in *The Lady's Not For Burning* Richard continued to take on a prodigious number of radio parts and poetry recitals besides starting at Pinewood Studios on his third film *Waterfront* and rehearsing another Christopher Fry play *The Boy With The Cart*.

It was only a one-act play, but a formidable task for its two central characters — Richard as the boy and seventy-two-year Mary Jerrold as the mother. Virtually alone they had to make the story of a shepherd boy, who hears a divine call and wheels his mother across England in a wheelbarrow to build a church with his bare hands, credible and deeply moving.

So daunting was the role that understudy Paul Daneman remember it as his worst moment in the theatre. 'Richard got influenza at the time of the first run-through and I was terrified at the prospect of taking over so soon. Happily he recovered in time for the opening. He had an extraordinary presence and quite fantastic repose. It was very unusual to see a young man walk on stage with all the maturity and quiet assurance of a middle-aged man. He seemed to know, either by experience or instinct, exactly what *not* to do. He came into a very middle-class theatre as a kind of regal peasant who would tell wonderful stories about Old Dai holding up the pit-prop with his bare hands and how his father stole food so that his sons could grow into the strongest in the valley.

'But it was strange how he tackled that part. At the first rehearsal he read beautifully and we were all impressed. But as we rehearsed for another six weeks — which was much too long — he never did another thing. We kept asking ourselves. "When is he going to do something?" We were all trying new things; yet he never did. And when we came to the first night, Richard's performance seemed to be exactly as it had been at the first rehearsal. But it was an enormous success. People came backstage with tears in their eyes and saying how moving his performance had been.'

Gielgud, who again directed, considers that Burton could not have been bettered. 'It was one of the most beautiful performances I had ever seen, and he and Mary Jerrold together were absolutely divine.

'It was a very simple miracle play that Fry had written for an amateur festival somewhere, and Richard's simplicity and shining sincerity were deeply moving. He knew himself how good he was in it, and he talks of it now with such affection as if it were his great moment and the part that made him into a star. But I don't remember it causing all that much of an impact in London. It was a charming play but it ran for only a few weeks at the Lyric, Hammersmith.'

Gielgud was right. It was strictly small fry compared with the richness and sophistication of the new *Venus Observed* which had just opened with Olivier at St James's, but in Richard's mind it had made him a star.

After three films, he had still to get a bad notice and at last the message that C.A. Lejeune, the most celebrated and respected of all film critics, had written in the *Observer* was getting through. After *Now Barabbas Was A Robber* she wrote: 'Mr Burton is an actor whose progress I shall watch with great curiosity. To my mind he has all the qualities of a leading man that the British film industry badly needs at this juncture: youth, good looks, a photogenic face, obviously alert intelligence, and a trick of getting the maximum effect with the minimum of fuss.' Korda signed Burton on a long-term contract at £100 a week.

With this guarantee Richard bought a house in Hampstead, but was shrewd enough to live in a self-contained upstairs flat and sub-let the rest of the house. He went into two more films, *Green Grow The Rushes* and *The Woman With No Name* , but this was his Fry period, and after an out of town production of *A Phoenix Too Frequent* he made his Broadway debut in *The Lady's Not For Burning*.

Five British films had failed to launch him as a major movie discovery. The Americans would need only one. Hollywood offers poured in, but he marked time. Korda still had him under contract. He still wanted the full accolade of the theatre. There was a proposal that he should play Romeo to Olivia de Havilland's Juliet on Broadway, but he surprisingly shied away from what would have been the most prestigious role of his career. The truth was that he regarded Romeo as 'an unbearable, prissy character'. His attitude, then, explains much of his personality now, and echoes the words of his confused young sweetheart in Taibach, 'Richie was never a toucher — never one of your gropers.' In a BBC interview he explained: 'I can't play with girls. I'm not a romantic actor in that sense. I think I'm recognised as a sort of sexual actor, but Romeo I've never played. That mawkish lover is beyond my capacity. Because the acting urge to kiss somebody on stage is beyond me. I can't do it. Because I can't bear to be touched, physically touched, on the stage or on the screen. It has to be very carefully arranged. I really can't bear to be touched and I rarely allow myself to touch other people — physically touch them, I mean. When I have to kiss a woman on stage or on the screen, horrors start up.'

The horrors were a long way from starting up when he returned to Stratford-on-Avon and the fame that had so far eluded him.

Chapter Eight

EVERYTHING THAT HAS to be said about Richard Burton's fantastic season at Stratford came after the curtain on 3 April 1951 when Kenneth Tynan said it all in the *Observer* — thirty odd years on, his judgment still stands as the finest appraisal of the style and grace of Burton the actor:

A shrewd Welsh boy shines out with greatness ... His playing of Prince Hal in *King Henry IV, Part I* turned interested speculation to awe almost as soon as he started to speak: in the first intermission the local critics stood agape in the lobbies. Burton is a still, brimming pool, running disturbingly deep; at twenty-five he commands repose and can make silence garrulous. His Prince Hal is never a roaring boy; he sits hunched or sprawled, with dark unwinking eyes; he hopes to be amused by his bully companions, but the eyes constantly muse beyond them into the time when he must steady himself for the crown. 'He brings his cathedral on with him,' said one dazed member of the company. For all his bold chivalry this watchful Celt seems surely to have strayed from a wayside pulpit. Fluent and sparing of gesture, compact and spruce of build, Burton smiles where other Hals have guffawed; relaxes where they have strained; and Falstaff (played with affectionate obesity by Anthony

Quayle) must work hard to divert him. In battle, Burton's voice cuts urgent and keen — always likeable, always inaccessible. If he can sustain and vary this performance through to the end of *Henry V*, we can safely send him along to swell the thin company of living actors who have shown us the mystery and the power of which heroes are capable.

Some say he didn't sustain the performance through to the end, including Burton himself. 'It really depressed me. The critics gave me a terrible roasting in the second part of *Henry*. They said I couldn't talk, couldn't walk, couldn't do anything well. Olivier told me, "Don't worry about it. The main thing is they took such a long time saying it."'

In fact the critics were quite kind. And Olivier was right. As P.L. Mannock said in the *Daily Herald*. 'I felt exactly the same about Olivier's *Henry V* at the Old Vic before the war. Feeling is there, and full expression will follow.'

Nevertheless, the season was a spectacular success. By late October, when the three stage kings took their final bows — Redgrave as Richard II, Harry Andrews as Henry IV, Burton as Henry V — more than 332,000 people had attended the theatre, pulling in a record £132,000. Richard's gain was £35 a week. Twenty-four hours later Richard was sailing with Sybil to New York to play the lead opposite Dorothy McGuire in Jean Anouilh's fantasy *Eurydice*. In London, where Dirk Bogarde took the lead, this *pièce noire* was entitled *Point of Departure*. On Broadway it was *Legend of Lovers*. The critics were enthusiastic about Richard. 'An actor of tremendous promise' — *The Herald Tribune*. 'Intelligent and persuasive' — *The New York Times*.

But generally they thought the production 'cheerless, cynical and muddled'. It opened at the Plymouth Theatre on Boxing Day and closed two weeks later. Noel Willman, who played Monsieur Henri, recalls: 'It was the classic example of an American management mucking up and mishandling an English production. Dorothy McGuire was simply not right for the role. She is a darling, and in many ways a good actress. But in this instance she was badly miscast.'

Hugh Griffith, who had played Shakespeare's 'great magician, damned Glendower', and had entertained Richard during the Stratford run, was the most demonstrative in his disgust. In fury he headed for Pier 90 to catch the Queen Mary back home. But when he arrived the docks were empty of ships and he reluctantly stalked back to his hotel. 'Hello,' said Burton. 'Thought you were going home.'

'Dammit,' growled Griffith. 'I'm not Jesus. I can't walk the bloody Atlantic.'

Richard shared his disenchantment. He called the production 'A Streetcar Named McGuire'.

But back in London his next play *Montserrat* received similar treatment. The critics praised the acting. The public stayed away. After the first night he was agreeably surprised to find he was playing to a full house. But after his praises had been sung in the dressing-room, he suddenly felt depressed and alone. He sauntered off to the pub across the road and was relieved to see one familiar face. His charming old friend Alan Badel who had shared his season at Stratford.

'What's yours?' said Burton.

'A Guinness.'

For a few minutes they stood in silence. Then a

thought dawned on Burton. 'Were you out front tonight, by any chance?'

'Yeah.'

Another long silence. 'Well, what did you think of it.'

Badel gave a non-committal shrug. 'All right.'

Richard could not resist the question any longer. 'What did you think of *me* then.'

Badel looked at him coldly. 'You need a haircut.'

Richard's disappointment was tempered with an irresistible offer from Twentieth Century-Fox — the promise of leading roles in three films at $50,000 a time. At the current rate of exchange the contract was worth £54,000.

Burton's style of living in Hollywood was contrary to all the known rules of tinsel town. Some regarded him as a peasant devoid of taste in clothes, food and wine. But others, particularly Humphrey Bogart, saw his lack of personal trappings, his borrowed cars and his flat on the wrong side of town, as the equipment of an eccentric extrovert who wasn't going to be tied into the system. They collided as twin personalities. Burton fitted Bogart's pattern. When they first met up Bogart said: 'It's unusual to get a trained actor out here. All these Ricks and Rocks used to work as gas station attendants. Go into any major studio and shout, "Fill her up", and all the leading men will come running.'

One of the Burtons' most regular guests was the ubiquitous Badel, then in Hollywood to play John the Baptist to Rita Hayworth's Salome. He detested the place, left after three months and never went back. 'I couldn't stand it. I really couldn't,' he told me before he died. 'And Richard wasn't very happy there at the

110

time either. My salient memory of that time is that they were terribly kind to me. Sybil was absolutely marvellous.

'Every Sunday we used to foregather at the Grangers. They had a very big house with an enormous swimming pool in the grounds. It was all very English — Deborah Kerr who was starring opposite Richard in *My Cousin Rachel*, Stewart Granger, Jean Simmons, Richard and Sybil, Michael Wilding, Elizabeth Taylor and others. I don't think Richard got to know Elizabeth very well then. He didn't seem to have very much to do with her. She used to sit with her feet dangling in the water, very pregnant, and alone. She was a loner, absolutely.'

On the set there was an uneasy relationship between the cut glass Miss de Havilland and the rough cut diamond from Wales, and yet they worked well together. Publicity stories quote her as saying: 'I shudder to think of the fame awaiting this young man. There isn't another leading man like him.'

The immediate fame Richard sought was the leading role in *The Robe*, the make or break epic that was to introduce CinemaScope, but while he was being considered he went into *The Desert Rats* and won the battle of Tobruk. He enjoyed working with James Mason, who played the skin-headed Rommel, and carousing with Robert Newton, cast in character as an alcoholic private.

One weekend Burton and Newton assumed American accents and crossed the border into Mexico without visas. 'We became absolutely paralysed with tequila,' says Richard. 'And on the way back we were so stoned that we completely forgot about our accents, and we landed in the pokey for the night.'

Towards the end of 1952 *My Cousin Rachel* was

released, and though many critics savaged the film the reaction to Burton was the same on both sides of the Atlantic. Hedda Hopper welcomed 'one of the most exciting actors I've seen in Hollywood in the past ten years.' C.A. Lejeune of the *Observer* confirmed her earlier opinion and saw him 'so closely resembling a fiery young Laurence Olivier that he is bound to set Hollywood ablaze.'

Burton's role in *My Cousin Rachel* brought him three press and magazine awards, an Oscar nomination and the coveted role of Marcellus in *The Robe*. He had something to celebrate and celebrate he did at Bogie's fifty-second birthday party on Christmas Day. He and Bogart were still at it when Mr and Mrs Charles Lederer threw a New Year's Party. He jumped on a piano and rhythmically recited speeches from a variety of Shakesperian plays while old-time musical star Jack Buchanan went into a tap-dancing routine and another guest banged out jazz on the keys beneath Burton's feet. When midnight struck he was kissing in 1953 with Jean Simmons, whom he would be starring with in *The Robe*.

Such was their passion that Sybil, as tolerant as any wife could be, walked purposefully to the centre of the floor, slapped his face and left. The Burtons, who had been house guests of Stewart Granger and Jean, moved out and rented a small house from Pamela Mason.

The *Saturday Evening Post* reported that Sybil had a fixed formula for dealing with her husband's affairs. 'The first week she tells him: "She's a nice girl; don't do anything to hurt her." The second week: "Richard, don't do anything to hurt us."

During the filming of *The Robe*, Emlyn Williams stayed with the Burtons and saw a great deal of Sybil.

But he and Richard scarcely met ... 'because I was at the theatre at night and Richard was up every morning at six to go to the studio. But there were two nights when Richard came to the Los Angeles theatre where we were playing Dickens, and this was marvellous of him because he had to work early next morning. Moreoever, he roped in many others: Lauren Bacall, Humphrey Bogart, Robert Newton, Clifton Webb — they all came backstage and were very nice. But I knew they didn't come of their own accord. That was real Welsh loyalty for you. But otherwise all I saw of Richard was an enormous pile of clothes left in the bathroom every day for Sybil to wash. Everything was covered in bole because he had been wearing togas and things and was caked in this brown stuff.'

The picture of Sybil as washerwoman confirmed her in the role of the supportive, maternal, all-sacrificing wife. 'You do become something of a nursemaid,' she said. 'You worry about his sleep and his health, the way you do with a child.' Whatever her view of Richard's obsession with Jean Simmons, who was also working late night at the studio, she kept her silence and seemed to accept his extra-marital adventures with the same aplomb that would later confound those who observed her quiet dignity and confidence during the height of the *Cleopatra* scandal. It was as if she saw his infidelity as a constant reassurance against his fear of a talent that he looked upon as the mistakenly bestowed gift of a careless god. All his seductions were of the mind. She had married him because he was a man of her own class moving up. She knew instinctively that all women did this, and for this reason she was aware that he was able to prove himself by impressing great beauties with the boastful vitality of a peasant who had become the prince of players.

His hidden insecurity was her outward strength.

Throughout this period Richard was continually compared to Olivier and was accused of selling out to Hollywood. But this was not strictly so. Richard came back from Hollywood to play a season at the Old Vic at the age of twenty-five while Olivier had made several films without remotely approaching the stardom of Burton, and was that much older when he appeared at the Vic and then took off for Hollywood to make *Wuthering Heights*.

Indeed Olivier was thiry-seven before he settled down to prolonged work in the 'classical' theatre. Yet the criticism is still levelled at Burton that he sacrificed his art to his ambition. It is an odd obsession of the precious few who have gained a certain notoriety by embalming themselves in the peculiar bachelor freemasonry of the theatre. Brando came from the stage, so did Bogart. Both were hailed on Broadway. Neither of them went back and neither were accused of turning their backs on the great white way.

What is forgotten is that Burton came back to play *Hamlet* as openers for Michael Benthal at £45 a week and, at the same time, suffering a tax loss of all but £6,000 of his £82,000 earnings from three Hollywood pictures.

His Dane wasn't too well received and neither was the performance of Claire Bloom, his on-stage Ophelia and backstage inamorata. The Prime Minister, Winston Churchill, liked it. During the second interval he wandered into Richard's dressing-room and rumbled: 'My Lord Hamlet. May I use your lavatory?' That night Burton took eighteen curtain calls and Churchill reportedly remarked that 'it was as exciting and virile a performance of *Hamlet* as I can remember.'

But the power of his performance, so appealing to Sir Winston, was interpreted by others as a weakness because it made the Prince too forceful a personality ever to be tormented by indecision.

This view was endorsed towards the end of its record-breaking run when Burton was visited by Sir John Gielgud. They were to take supper after the show and Richard recalls how 'I was trying to hurry but was continually being held up by well-wishers, hangers-on and freeloaders. John got bored and suddenly said: "Well, dear boy, shall I go ahead or shall I wait until you are better — um, er, I mean ready?" The truth was out. John was infamous for putting his foot in it. Later Gielgud confirmed to me what he called 'My little indiscretion'.

Burton frankly described himself at that time as 'The Tommy Steele of the Old Vic'. But if he won the young fans' popular vote he missed the purists' approval. He then took on the extra strain of *Coriolanus* and here he did achieve a truly memorable performance. The role of the eloquent Roman noble with its succession of heroic speeches suited his technique admirably. Olivier generously told him that no one else could ever play the part now, and the first night confirmed his position as the new idol of the cultured bobbysoxers. In the gallery they were screaming for him — just as they used to call for 'Larry' years ago. John Neville, who has done more Shakespeare with Richard than anyone, judges *Coriolanus* to be one of his really great achievements.

One man carries a personal reminder of the vigour with which Richard attacked that role — Paul Daneman who played Tullus Aufidius. In the final scene a Third Conspirator tells Aufidius, 'Let him feel your sword.'

'Richard was terribly proud of his skill with the sword,' says Daneman. 'He used to tell me how the stuntman had fought him in *The Robe* and had gone beserk, attacking him like a lunatic; and yet he had managed to hold him off. Well, I rather fancy myself with a sword as well. We rehearsed our fight scenes very fully and Richard was terribly keen. "We'll make the sparks fly," he said. We had short Roman swords, no gloves, and the lighting was very low. Anyway, in our enthusiasm, we fought rather too furiously, and I suddenly felt a tremendous wallop around the knuckles. I was carried off in some pain and then the hand went numb, and it wasn't until I was at the bottom of the steps underneath the stage that I saw my hand was streaming with blood. The nurse at the theatre bound it up and we finished the performance.

'Later I went to Charing Cross Hospital and found that the blow had cut through the tendon of the index finger of the right hand. For the next six weeks I had to go on stage wearing this bloody great plaster, and I was still wearing it when we were playing *Twelfth Night*. I still can't completely bend that finger. After that it became a firm rule at the Old Vic that gloves should always be worn for sword fights.'

Besides five Shakesperian roles, Burton undertook the first BBC radio broadcast of *Under Milk Wood* as a tribute to the late Dylan Thomas who had died from booze in New York the previous year. He played the First Narrator in a cast that included Hugh Griffith as blind Captain Cat, Sybil as Miss Myfanwy Price of the loving hot-water-bottled body, and Phil Burton and Rachel Roberts taking several parts. He also joined in public readings on behalf of the trust fund for the education of Dylan's children, and during one evening of homage at the Globe Theatre, reading with Dame

Edith Evans, Hugh Griffith and Emlyn Williams, he wept unashamedly on stage as he read *Fern Hill*.

Richard deeply mourned the passing of that wild, strangely inspired Welshman whose earthy genius filled him with awe, and he was shattered when the poet died prematurely in his fortieth year. He remembered how Dylan had stayed with him and Sybil at Hampstead during his last year and had 'sometimes treated me like a dog — he absolutely dismissed me unless he wanted something'. And there was the sad, lingering memory of that October day when Dylan telephoned him from Phil Burton's London flat wanting to borrow £200.

'What do you want if for?' asked Richard.

'For the education of my children,' said the self-styled 'podgy pub-crawler' who added up money like he did his backward spelling of his famous village of Llareggub.

'Come off it,' said Richard. 'Don't give me that.'

'All right then. For two hundred quid I'll give you the rights in my new play.'

'Oh yes. Where is it?'

'Well I haven't actually written it yet,' said Dylan. 'It's the love story of an affair between two streets.'

In recalling their last dialogue today Burton feels a certain guilt towards a man of such tremendous talent. 'He held me spellbound on the phone while he spun an extraordinary story of these two streets. But something inside me told me that it didn't ring true as a drama penned; some dark suspicion that for all the brilliance and fluency, he was making the whole thing up as he went along. Anyway, I didn't have the money. I suppose I could have sold something, but I didn't and he didn't get the £200 and immediately afterwards he went to America and the next month he was dead. I've had a conscience about it ever since.

'Apart from Behan, he was the only true Bohemian I had met. If he wore old clothes, it was because he had no others. And as a joke he would hire a dress suit, bury it in the garden, dig it up again, and return it. He was always in drink, but never drunk when he was writing. I wanted to be a writer more than anything else, I still do. You know how Dylan used to write? On bits of brown paper. He would stick them up on the walls. His room was a wallpaper of poetry. He saw my *Hamlet* at the Old Vic three times — but he only saw the third act each time. He hated intervals, and he told me that he would walk in with the crowds after the second interval and get a free seat. He never got caught. I was his bewitched hanger-on.'

Burton took another eighteen-month break from the Old Vic for another three American movies — *The Prince of Players* (1954), in Hollywood, *The Rains of Ranchipur* (1955) with Lana Turner and *Alexander The Great* (1956) in Spain with Claire Bloom and Stanley Baker (a reminder of the Rattigan play when Stanley carried a spear and Richard got the sack). But his return to the Old Vic brought about a kind of Beatlemania to Waterloo Road. John Neville had become the Old Vic's idol while Richard was away. That season one half of the house cheered every entrance and exit by Neville; the other half vociferously supported the visiting star.

'It was incredible,' says Neville. 'Those crowds were really enormous, stretching right across the road and blocking the way from Waterloo Station. They screamed and wore all sorts of things such as scarves and jumpers with our names on.' It was natural that these two men should gain rival factions. One was a film star and a miner's son; the other a lorry driver's son who had turned down a movie contract to stay at the Old Vic. Richard was a fiery Celt; dark, stocky, green-eyed. John was the studious, soft spoken Englishman; tall, lean, fair and blue-eyed. Both were thirty years old — charming and handsome.

'The first manifestation of this sort of hysteria was when Johnnie Ray came over here,' says Neville. 'But to say I was trying to compete with Richard, as some critics suggested, was absolute balls. I certainly don't look upon acting as a competition, and Richard and I were always great friends. Yet there was still this invented rivalry between us, and it seemed to us that many of the critics were preoccupied by this aspect raher than by the plays.'

Burton's development in the role of *Henry V* was noted by Tynan: 'By stressing the gentle gamester aspect of the part and delivering the rest as a trumpet voluntary, many actors have been able to blind us to the barbarity of Henry. Richard Burton takes a steeper path. He gives us a cunning warrior, stocky and astute, unafraid of harshness or of curling the royal lip. The gallery gets no smiles from him, and the soldiery none but the scantiest commiseration. Though it sometimes prefers rant to exuberance, this is an honest performance, true and watchful and ruthless.'

Richard's *Henry V* won him the coveted *Evening Standard* Drama Award for the best performance by an actor in 1955. At thirty, he had arrived triumphant in the theatre. But this was not all. In February he and Neville alternated in the roles of Othello and Iago on successive nights. It was the toughest and most exhausting work that either actor had ever tackled.

At first Neville hesitated to accept the challenge. 'In a sense it meant that we were rehearsing two plays,

119

two enormous classical roles, in six weeks. Normally you would get four weeks to rehearse one play. We did both in six weeks; moreover, we didn't have a week between the openings. We opened one night and swapped parts the next. Neither of us really had enough time to study, but it was easier for me in a way. I was originally asked to play Iago and so we rehearsed it that way for three weeks. Now, Iago is one of the longest parts in all Şhakespeare and it has the added difficulty of being predominantly in prose which is far harder to learn than Shakespeare's verse. So I got the more difficult part out of the way first. It was just Richard's bad luck. He was marvellous in both roles, but when it came to rehearsing the other way round he was put under the greater strain. I always thought he was a little behind in his learning, not through any fault of his own, but simply by force of circumstance. Certain things in Iago are fiendishly difficult to learn. For instance there's the famous street scene where he kills Rodrigo — a great mix-up in semi-darkness, and it's a bloody awful scene to learn. Iago is the *deus ex machina* there; he simply has to keep going. And Richard had to do this on the last part of our rehearsals.'

Burton's financial position had improved since he refused Dylan the loan, but it was peculiar and not entirely understood by his critics. He had the gross income of a Hollywood star — as much as £50,000 for a film taking no more than three months — yet he did not live like one. In California he and Sybil rented a simple two-bedroomed house without a swimming pool and hired a utilitarian car. He said they had calculated that, with extreme economy, it was possible to survive in Hollywood on as little as £35 a week. They were certainly well in pocket from their

£140 a week living allowance from the studio. He wasn't exactly a big spender and many thought he had a serious impediment in his reach. His excuse was: 'They like you to spend a lot of money in Hollywood because that way you get dependent on them and then they can do what they like with you. But I didn't want to be dependent on anyone.' And that was partly true, even though friends in Hollywood suffered from his parsimonious hospitality and his casual use of their expensive facilities. No one could manipulate the canny Celt.

He believed, as he still does, in putting back what you have taken out. When Frank Hauser was forming Meadow Players to reopen the Oxford Playhouse and desperately needing funds, he went along to the Old Vic to ask Burton if he would help him by appearing in a production. To his amazement, Richard gave him £2,000 instead. 'It was by far the biggest donation and it was what enabled us to launch the company.'

Yet, as Hauser says, Burton was not really super-rich at this time. So long as he had a residence in Britain, or visited the country for more than six months in any fiscal year, he would be fully liable to income tax. Disregarding all the many tax deductable expenses, it meant that as a married man without children he was liable to pay over £42,000 tax on an income of £50,000 a year. To a hedonist who for the most part worked to live rather than lived to work this made little sense.

He made one more film in the summer of 1957 — *Seawife* — and moved to a house near Lake Geneva as a tax exile. Joan Collins was his co-star. Later she was to say that she turned down Burton's offer of seduction and gave her favours to a well endowed lad who fetched for the camera crew.

121

Oddly enough she was living with Arthur Loew Jr, who later befriended Elizabeth Taylor after Mike Todd's death. She left him for Nicky Hilton, Elizabeth's first husband. It would have made a sad enactment of *La Ronde* had she succumbed to Burton. But who was to know how many times the partners were changed in the constant merry-go-round of Hollywood love?

Chapter Nine

WHEN THE BURTONS moved into Le Pays de Galles, their Swiss tax exile in Celigny, Sybil found herself pregnant and Richard sent for his brother Ivor and his wife Gwen. But hardly had they finished celebrating the happy news, that Sybil had waited for for eight years, than their joy was shadowed by the death of Daddy Ni.

Dic-the-son-of-a-carpenter had seen eighty-one years — fifty of them as a working collier — and only one of his son's pictures. And he didn't sit all the way through that. 'As soon as he saw Richie pour himself a drink on screen, he said 'That's that, that's it,' and he was away for a pint. Hilda told me: 'He wasn't a film-going man and he thought *My Cousin Rachel* was disgusting. All that love making. He couldn't grasp that they were acting. He kept saying, "What the hell is all this kissing?" and when my eldest brother Tom explained it was only acting, he said: "Acting to damned. It looks real enough to me." He never could understand the film business.'

But perhaps he did. For the day after his granddaughter Kate was born on 11 September 1957, his son Richard flew to New York for Anouilh's *Time Remembered* and to give his teenage juvenile lead a time she would never forget.

Years later Susan Strasberg wrote of their passionate love in a rented cold water apartment and told of her happy giddiness in being introduced to Olivier, who was appearing in John Osborne's *The Entertainer*, as his own 'Baby Angel'. She was overjoyed to have been given a white mink scarf and muff for Christmas, but miffed when she saw the full length mink he bought for Sybil. Was it a conscience present? Miss Strasberg doesn't say.

But Burton made no secret of the intimacy of his relationship. She met Phil Burton, now living in New York, and she found Richard 'more comfortable and less theatrical in his presence'. To members of his family who were visiting from Wales she was his 'pocket princess' and he made her show off her Welsh and expose their relationship. 'I gazed into his green eyes and recited the words he had taught me.

"Who do you love?" he asked.

"Ti," I said. "Rwyn dy garu di." (I love you)

"Faint?" he queried.

"Mwy na neb arall yn y byd," I replied (More than anyone else in the world)!'

With Susan it was all fresh and she really loved him more than anyone else in the world. She was captivated by his 'charisma and charm' and so, apparently, was her father, Lee Strasberg, the founder and artistic director of the New York Actors' Studio, when she took him home to show him off. Her parents were greatly amused by his tumble of yarns including the one about his grandfather and Black Sambo.

But Susan was worried about the occasional stumbles into black despair. He wrote to her of his fear of dying from the booze and told her between wild bursts of poetry 'without the alcohol, when I'm cold sober, I feel I belong to a university town somewhere, teaching literature or drama to grubby little boys, Christ! What if I bore the piss out of everybody when I'm sober?'

He never was.

The last big party in New York came in May when Lord Olivier, Sir Laurence as he was by now, entertained 200 celebrities in a midnight cruise up the Hudson and Richard arrived in a red jersey with 'HMS *Olivier*' written across his chest. It was a wonderful Cockney-style outing, with barrels of stout and a buffet of jellied eels and fish and chips served in English newspapers, and as Richard pounded the deck in a wild version of 'Knees-up-Mother Brown' he bumped into the actor who had become famous as England's angry young playwright. The man was John Osborne who, like Richard, had a Welsh father and a barmaid mother and whose play *Look Back In Anger* said everything that Richard felt about the intolerant class-structure of English society.

Osborne had created a new anti-hero in the rough shape of Jimmy Porter — an intellectual from the slums who spat on English china. It had been a brilliant success in the theatre but, despite the acclaim afforded to Kenneth Haigh in the stage production, it needed a bigger name for the screen version.

Burton was an obvious choice for the part. But would he grab the chance? So often he had lost all sense of direction in Hollywood. There were plans for him to appear with Carroll (Baby Doll) Baker in *The Miracle* and in yet another epic with Gina Lollobrigida, *Solomon and Sheba*. Also Milton Sperling, the Hollywood producer who had brought him to New York for *Time Remembered*, had signed him to star in *The Bramble Bush*. But for once

Burton's judgment was sound; he recognised the Jimmy Porter role as offering him the best of both worlds of cinema and theatre — a film in which the basic ingredients of the stage play would not be lost by transfer to the screen.

In August 1958, after a two-month holiday in Switzerland with Sybil and baby Kate, Richard returned to Britain to start work on the film. It was his first visit as an overseas resident and his newfound wealth was obvious. They had a nanny for the baby, he had part ownership of a Swiss bank, and when he drove back to Pontrhydyfen it was at the wheel of a £6,000 Rolls-Royce. He talked proudly about his beautiful villa, of the luxurious convertible he had left behind, of the oodles of dollars he had earned from eight Hollywood movies, and the £100,000 he had under his number in his own bank. 'I need never work again,' he told friends.

The miners knew all about Burton the film star and they were proud of him, but it wasn't their way to treat him as anything special. They liked his 'posh roller' though; and Sam the Drop, whose idol was Pierrepoint and whose one great ambition in life was to become the public hangman, climbed into the back of the car and just sat there for hours, feeling the leather, examining the dashboard, and then sinking back and tugging at the hand-strap and dreaming of ropes and trap doors. It was quite an event to see him *outside* a pub during opening hours for Sam the Drop was also known as Sam the Schooner, and his passion for the local 'iron ore' was so great that he had even shocked the agnostic miners by trying to sell his parents' gravestone to raise beer money. 'Would you like me to drive you somewhere, Sam?' the film star asked. 'Ooh no, Richie. I'll just sit here and enjoy myself.'

On the other side of the road Richard spotted the unmistakable, shuffling figure of old Will Dai, and knowing he was always good for a laugh he crossed over. ''ello,' said Will, peering out from beneath the drooping peak of his button-down cap. 'W-w-well, if it isn't b-b-bloody D-d-douglas F-f-fairbanks 'imself.' His stutter was worse than ever, and he looked unusually glum.

'Hello,' said Richard. 'How are things going then?'

'It's t-t-terrible,' said Will. 'I've l-lost-s-s-seventy-f-five th-thousand p-p-pounds.'

'However could that happen?'

'W-well, I had s-s-seven d-d-draws on the f-f-football p-pools. And j-just one t-team let me down.'

'Really? Which team was that?'

'Fuh-fuh-fuh ...'

'Fulham?' suggested Richard.

N-n-no. Fuh-fuh-fuh ...'

'Falkirk?'

Will grinned wickedly. 'No-n-no. Fuh-fuh-fuhking Swansea.'

Richard accompanied him into brother Tom's local, The Copper House and became just 'Jenks' again as the public bar chat burped on about the unforgettable exploits of the Cwmavon Boys School 'Wonder Team' that never conceded a point in three full seasons in the thirties and scored over a thousand against.

'Remember Richie. Unbeatable they were in League and Cup, and there was a prize of a gold watch and a holiday in Porthcawl for every member of any team that scored against them. Bloody geniuses some of those little buggers were. Remember Viv Allen then, Richie? He was one of Phil Burton's little actors. But duw! What a scrum-half! Fast as greased lightning! Remember when they played your old team, Meredith Jones's Eastern, and Viv came up against young Joe Drew who was slow off the mark and Viv flattened him every time they got the strike? And he was giving him such a hammering that old Ma Drew ran on the pitch and belted him across the ear'ole with her brolly.'

Richard remembered and his thoughts wandered ruefully into wondering how he could ever scrum down again in a Number 8 shirt with millions to be lost at the crack of a collar bone.

As he frequented his favourite pubs in London there was a suspicion that he missed the British way of life. But he insisted that Switzerland had a lot more going for it than cuckoo clocks. He had plenty of British neighbours like Deborah Kerr and Alistair MacLean; he could swim and ski, and if he wanted to watch rugby there was a fine team nearby at Grenoble. Paris was only forty-five minutes away, Rome just a couple of hours. As for Sybil, he said, she much preferred it because she didn't get hay fever.

Britain, however, can react waspishly towards those who have deserted her for tax reasons. He argued his case soundly enough: 'If I make three pictures in a year I would earn about £100,000, and in England I'd pay £93,000 of that in tax. But now I'm a Geneva resident all I pay is £700. Do you wonder that I don't want to live in London again? Ours is an uncertain profession. We make a lot of money for a few years — then nothing.'

He spoke frankly about Britain's 'vicious, punitive tax situation' and expressed the wish that someone like Olivier would leave and 'really shake the Chancellor of the Exchequer'. Unfortunately, people took him too seriously when he remarked: 'I'm not against high taxes for Britain. I believe everyone should pay them; except actors.' After that remark the criticism mounted sharply. He didn't care.

He thought the whole thing was a game and that Hollywood was a toy town. 'An enchanted city where every moment you think you're going to wake up to reality. It's a great place for a short visit, but a disturbing place for long stays. You would forget there were any poor people in the world. You would forget how to walk. Even to go one hundred yards from one studio to another, people take cars.'

And he was refreshingly honest about his attitude to films. 'At one Hollywood party I heard director Billy Wilder refer to actors as "a pack of bums". Bogie got mad over that. Anyway, I asked Wilder to explain his remark, and he said, "Look, I can photograph Gregory Peck's face from four different angles, put them into a film anywhere I like and make them mean anything I choose." And you know, I had to admit he was right. I'm strictly in Hollywood for the fame films bring, especially the money. But I don't take films that seriously. The theatre is magic, but somehow I can't believe in films. It all seems a bit of a lark.'

He was about to start another lark off screen, but at this stage he badly needed some worthwhile achievement to restore his popularity, and his part in *Look Back in Anger* fitted the bill very well. The role of Jimmy Porter, the intellectual barrow-boy who sneers at the middle-class background of his wife, was tailor-made for him. Moreover, he had a first-rate director in Tony Richardson, who would later win an Oscar for *Tom Jones* and he was working with three top actresses: Dame Edith Evans, Mary Ure — then Osborne's wife — and most familiar of all, Claire Bloom who had shared hundreds of Old Vic nights with him, tours from the provinces to the battlements of Elsinore, and on through the campaigns of Alexander.

In mid-September, they were busy filming in the drab East End of London, lunching each day at workmen's caffs on faggots and pease pudding, but they were attracting precious little publicity.

The showbusiness columns were now dominated by the continuing story of the Taylor-Fisher-Reynolds 'triangle'. Six months earlier Elizabeth Taylor had been widowed by Mike Todd's air crash. Now all sympathy had passed; she was being pilloried in the world's press over her romance with Eddie Fisher and blamed for the breaking up of his story-book marriage to Debbie Reynolds. The Fishers' wedding had been running into troubled waters before Liz came on the scene. But no matter, Richard had his own problems.

Susan Strasberg was still madly in love with him and flew in from Brussels. Richard sent a studio car to meet her, but when she arrived in his dressing-room he was oddly flustered and bundled her into his john. She was bewildered.

'But I don't want to go to the bathroom,' she protested. 'It was so unexpected that I could not comprehend what he was asking'.

What the agitated Burton was telling her was, Claire Bloom was on her way to discuss the next scene.

Then the penny dropped, but not quite.

Finger to his lips Burton was trying to close the door. 'Oh I see,' said little Susan who didn't see at all at the time. 'You're afraid Claire will call Sybil if she sees me here. But why should she care?'

Poor Susan was left locked in the lavatory listening and peeping at the keyhole.

Later Richard comforted her and took her for a drink in an out of the way Elstree pub before driving her back to her hotel. No. He had better not come up for a drink in the Savoy. 'Someone might see us.' It was the brush off.

Susan was heartbroken. She walked through the autumn mists of the embankment. She stood on Waterloo Bridge and contemplated suicide. Next morning, with the resilience of a nineteen-year-old, she was winging back to Brussels and another love.

Claire never contemplated suicide. When Burton cut her dead, during out of studio hours in the making of their last film together, *The Spy Who Came In From The Cold*, she said: 'He hadn't changed at all, except physically, but that was natural as he was older. He was still drinking, he was still boasting, still reciting the same poems and telling the same stories.'

When Richard returned to Hollywood after the making of *Look Back In Anger* he began to behave like a fully-fledged star. He demanded and got twin Cadillacs — one for himself, one for the family — and insisted on having the best dressing-room in the studio. 'I'm not worth it, but it impresses.'

Inevitably, too, he became the subject of gossip. Publicity seeking starlets clung to him tighter than their minks and when Sybil was back in Switzerland, preparing for the arrival of her second baby (Jessica), he was asked about a rumour that he planned to take his latest teenage actress to Europe.

'It's true all right,' said Burton. 'I'm crazy about her and so is my wife.'

What was true was his cheerful indifference to consequence and his devastating effect on women. Actor Fredric March counted on his fingers and shrugged. 'Richard had a terrific way with women. I don't think he has missed half a dozen.'

When Richard was co-starring with Raymond Massey in *Prince of Players* the sardonic actor was asked if there was any woman Richard Burton failed to win.

'Yes. Marie Dressler,' Massey said.

'But she's dead.'

'Yes, I know.'

Producer Frank Ross called Burton 'A born male coquette.'

'He has the marvellous quality of making a woman feel as if she's the only one in the world worth talking to, and it's bliss, it really is,' said Lee Remick.

'I was madly in love with him for at least four days,' said Tammy Grimes. 'He makes women feel beautiful.'

He was now committed to films far below the merit of *Look Back In Anger*. The first was the totally forgettable *The Bramble Bush*, co-starring Barbara Rush. He called it 'a scramble with Rush' and without too much debate it was the worst film he ever made. The only consolation to the studio was that it was made on a small budget and wasn't a financial disaster.

The same could not be said about the second film, *Ice Palace*, a Warner Brothers version of Edna Ferber's outsize novel about feuding families in Alaska. It was absurdly long and, much to Burton's financial profit, ran far into overtime. His co-stars were Robert Ryan, Martha Hyer, Carolyn Jones and a great drink pal, Jim Backus. None of them emerged from this monstrous misconception of a movie with their reputations more sadly tarnished than Burton.

Questioned about the most important lesson he had learned from these pictures he replied: 'If you're going to make rubbish — be the best rubbish in it. I keep telling Larry Olivier that. It is no good playing a minor role in an epic like *Spartacus* which he's just done. Larry had a dressing-room half the size of Tony Curtis' on that film. And he got half Curtis' money. Well that's ridiculous. You've got to swank in Hollywood.'

In adopting this approach to movie-making he was simply playing the Hollywood survival game according to the age-old rules — never sell yourself short, never allow yourself to be upstaged by other stars; never concede privileges once gained; never be obviously tractable.

Vanity didn't enter into it. For the canny Celt it was essentially a matter of economic truths. He would prefer not to make rubbish, but pride in the films he made was no substitute for cash in the bank, and for him the number of zeros on the pay-cheque was a more reliable measure of success than the column inches of critical acclaim.

All the high-faluting talk of the artistic merit of *Look Back In Anger* left him cold. Film-making remained, in his eyes, a craft and nothing more, and he was strictly in it for the loot.

Given the opportunity to rest from movies without financial loss, he would gladly take it.

'But where else can you get that kind of money?' he asked.

The answer was on Broadway in *My Fair Lady* with a fee of $1,400 a week for his first year, and with the promise of $2,800 a week if he stayed on for a second year.

We are back where we started.

It was 1964. I had told the world he would marry Elizabeth Taylor and they were doing just that in the

Royal Suite at Montreal's Ritz Carlton Hotel. He was thirty-eight. Elizabeth was thirty-two.

I met up with them in New York. He was playing *Hamlet*, I was covering the Harlem riots. I don't know which was the more frightening experience.

Chapter Ten

RATHER IN THE same manner in which he had become accidentally involved with Elizabeth Taylor, though in no small measure due to a compelling buck'o'boy urge to meet any challenge (such as the dare thrown down by the cast of *Camelot* who thought this particular Cleopatra beyond his rakish strut), Richard found himself facing the consequence of his outrageous philandering in the naked glare of the footlights.

For on the day of his private and quiet wedding, almost two years to the day when Eddie Fisher gave public confirmation of his bedding of Elizabeth, he appeared on the stage of the opulent O'Keefe Centre in Toronto declaiming 'I say, we will have no more marriages.'

This *Hamlet* was to become his most spectacular stage success, yet the production which re-established him as a serious actor was an unplanned, accidental child of impulse and chance, conceived during the filming of *Becket* when Sir John Gielgud was called in as an emergency replacement to play the King of France. They were then shooting on location in Newcastle, and it so happened, that Gielgud was appearing locally in an ill-fated play *The Ides of March*.

Richard and Elizabeth went along to see the play and afterwards at the Station Hotel, Sir John asked what he was doing the following year for Shakespeare's quarter-centenary. Richard had no intention of joining in Shakespeare's birthday celebrations. Safe in the knowledge that Peter O'Toole was to play Hamlet at the National for Olivier he said: 'Oh, someone wants me to do Hamlet in New York.'

He saw that Sir John looked interested and for some reason, to this day Richard doesn't know why, he suddenly said: 'I'll only do it if you'll direct it.'

Sir John says: 'I thought it was some kind of joke but I agreed and I really thought nothing would ever come of it. I rather gathered that Richard had done it as a kind of dare to some American or other and had thought no more about it until he met me, and then rather casually got himself involved.'

Perhaps it was Elizabeth who persuaded him. It was her suggestion that he played the priest rather than the king in Becket and she was enjoying the role of the 'little woman' following her man. She hadn't worked since *VIPs* and during the making of *The Night of the Iguana* she had brought him a hot lunch to the set every day and fussed over his hair.

'Whatever the reason,' says Sir John, 'I must say that once he took it on he was extremely enthusiastic and never ran it down or slacked in any way even though we had to rehearse in bizarre circumstances.'

It was just as well that Richard was adamant about not wanting to wear doublet and hose. 'In tights my legs look like a pair of stockings idly thrown over a bed rail.' This perfectly suited Gielgud since he had long harboured the notion of doing *Hamlet* as a final rehearsal run-through and the circumstances surrounding the actual rehearsals didn't lend itself to actors wearing Elizabethan costumes. Though the town had only three newspapers, there were always at least fifty reporters hovering in the background, watching Richard and Elizabeth's every move, even noting the food they ate and the liquor they drank. Photographers were everywhere, and always there were the hordes of fans and demonstrators outside the King Edward Hotel where they sheltered in the viceregal suite, which members of the company called 'the zoo'.

Gielgud cannot recall rehearsing in more peculiar surroundings. 'It was most extraordinary. Richard and Elizabeth had to exercise her dogs on the roof because they couldn't go out on the street. And it was rather sad to see them in the hotel, holed up in the suite with a man with a machine-gun in the corridor. It made it very difficult to get him alone, and even when I went out to lunch with him between rehearsals there'd be four or five of the entourage sitting at adjoining tables, preventing people coming up and talking to him. When I said, "Please this is my lunch," Richard said, "No, no. They'll pay." And we sailed out and the entourage were left to pay the bill, which rather embarrassed me. I did ask them once to supper in Toronto, and it was the cheapest entertaining I ever did. I invited them to a steak house after the play and we had a marvellous supper with a lot of champagne. We were about ten or fifteen people, but when I asked for the bill the management wouldn't give me one, and when we came out there were two hundred people in the snow, waiting to see them drive away. The next morning I went back to tip the waiters at least, and they said, "No, no, no, we were paid so much extra by the proprietor last night that we wouldn't dream of taking a penny." So I was never able to be host to them in a proper way and, of course, that tremendous princeliness does isolate you in a funny way. I felt sorry I couldn't get to know them better, in a more intimate way, because of all the hoo-ha that was going on in the newspapers every time they put their noses outside the door.

'I thought it a great strain on their relationship and on their relationship with all the company. And I thought Richard handled that marvellously. He was very popular with the company. He took great pains to be nice to everybody. But it must have been a great strain for him, and it wasn't my idea of really working as one likes to do at rehearsals — intimately, privately, without the glare of publicity. Of course the management in some way rather liked it because it meant this enormous, fantastic success they had everywhere with the play.'

Enormous and *fantastic* was no exaggeration. In Toronto it grossed over $400,000 in four weeks. Richard, on fifteen per cent of the gross, picked up $60,000 — a remarkable sum for a pre-Broadway warm-up — and this was in 1964. The opening at Boston's Schubert Theatre was even more encouraging. He received standing ovations, excellent notices and the two weeks put another $21,000 in his pocket from the $140,000 take — the maximum possible with all standing-room sold.

But, as they say in showbiz, 'nobody hadn't seen nutting yet'. In New York it was a smash-hit unlike any other in the history of American Shakespearean productions. The success of Burton's plain-clothes *Hamlet* was incredible, unprecedented, mystifying. He broke the record for the greatest number of *Hamlet* performances on Broadway — reaching 136 compared with the 132 previously shared by Gielgud and Maurice Evans — and played to 204,000 people who paid near on one and half million dollars during the seventeen-week run to the Lunt-Fontanne Theatre. A special filming process enabled it to be shown at 1,000 movie houses and allowed his stage *Hamlet* to be preserved for posterity. It boosted the gross takings to a staggering $6,000,000 and gave Burton $900,000 in the bank.

This was more money than he had got for *Cleopatra* ($250,000), *VIPs* ($500,000), *Becket* ($250,000) and *The Night of the Iguana* ($500,000). Elizabeth had earned $2,000,000 for *Cleopatra* and *VIPs* so, at this stage, Richard was the top breadwinner with nearly half a million up on his new missus.

If 'ice' is the vulgar vernacular for diamonds then this was but the tip of the diamondberg. When I caught up with them in New York they were, after a month of marriage and two years of togetherness, a body corporate rather than coital bodies as far as their financial advisers were concerned. Richard boasted that he was a dollar millionaire and Elizabeth was in debt when they met in Rome. He was fond of saying that he had given all his wealth to Sybil and had started again from scratch with poor Liz. Certainly his generosity to his family was confirmed by Sybil's friends. It may have been encouraged by Elizabeth to remove all suspicions of cupidity and to present their love as a naked child without pockets for money. But her opulence belied such a poetic notion and exposed the child as one of illusion and themselves as the parents of disillusion. The plain fact was they had drawn up a business contract in Mexico before signing the marriage certificate in Canada. It probably accounted for him turning up half sloshed at his wedding. Elizabeth tried to sober him up and wondered aloud, 'I don't know why he is so nervous, after all we've been sleeping together for two years.'

His nervousness had more to do with the boardroom than the bedroom. For while he was filming *The Night of the Iguana* he was persuaded by their lawyer Aaron Frosch to agree to a complication of trusts that would shield future earnings from tax and protect their joint investments. If Elizabeth was in debt when Richard met her it was cleverness on her part that led him into the mistake of thinking she had fallen into the ways of a feminine Micawber.

She was far from that. At this time she still owned forty per cent of all rights to *Around the World in 80 Days* and because of her deal with Fox she had hauled in another $6,000,000 from *Cleopatra*. Marrying Burton also gave her the chance of renouncing her American citizenship and enjoying the tax privileges of a British subject living outside England.

She had locked him in taffeta with a wedding ring, but there was no doubting her love. If anything it was too obsessive, too demanding. She was always by his side. Everything he owed to her, but everything she attributed to his genius. Every night except Sundays, literally thousands of fans would mass around the corner of Broadway and 46th Street to catch a glimpse of them entering and leaving the Lunt-Fontanne Theatre and it was an incredible ritual which became a recognised feature of the New York scene.

Around 11.30 each night they would emerge from the theatre under a large marquee. Teenagers squealed and screamed, the great crowd pressed forward against the police barriers. Seconds later a limousine, flanked by mounted police, pulled away and the great parade was over for another night. *Time*

140

magazine judged it to be the 'fastest, flashiest show around'.

One night I shared the extraordinary experience. As we left the theatre together, the crowd, hot and sticky and stained in the tropical night, surged towards us and made the great canyon of skyscrapers boom and echo with a mighty roar. Shirt-sleeved police with revolvers swinging bare on their hips cleared a path for us to reach the car. Then the crowd broke through the linked arms of the police and Elizabeth lost her shoe. She smiled but hurried on. Split-second timing was needed to escape the Lunt-Fontanne. As we drove off, Richard pointed out a bar across the street. 'It's a good place to drink but to reach it we have to drive around four or five blocks and approach it discreetly from the opposite direction.'

I had been to Harlem covering the riots and apologised for not getting back in time for the whole play. 'I guessed as much,' said Richard. 'You smell like an air raid. I heard on the radio they had fire hoses out and the place was burning. It's amazing to think that a real bloody battlefront is just up the road while we are caught up in another madness. It's a weird city.'

'I'd rather be there,' I said. 'At least they gave me a tin hat. Why don't you come down and have a look? We'll drop Elizabeth off at the hotel and then we can have a couple of jars at P.J. Clarke's afterwards.'

Elizabeth who was sitting next to me jabbed me where it hurts and said, 'Watch it buster. You two are going nowhere.'

'Sorry old love,' said Richard. 'It's not the riots she's worried about, it's PJ's.'

Many old wounds were healing now, and no reconciliation pleased Richard more than his reunion with the man most responsible for his development as an actor — his foster-father Philip Burton. It was not easily achieved since *le scandale* had driven a splintery wedge between the two men. Phil Burton had loathed all public exposure of Richard's private life, and he had felt compelled to side with Sybil during the *Cleopatra* affair. Moreover he had been directly embarrassed by the Burton–Taylor romance. On the day after a US Congressman proposed that Richard should be banned from the States on moral grounds his second 'father' was facing his examination for American citizenship. The examiner somehow regarded this issue as being relevant to the applicant's fitness to become an American, but happily it did not influence the final decision. The application was passed.

It was Elizabeth, acting on her own initiative, who finally brought Burton senior and junior back together. During rehearsals of *Hamlet*, when Richard was in a highly nervous state, she swallowed her pride and boldly telephoned the man she had never met, the man she knew must feel hostile towards her.

'Richard needs you,' she said. 'Please come.'

Subsequently, Philip Burton spoke to Sybil and she agreed he ought to go to Richard if he needed him. So the father–son relationship was restored. Philip Burton was charmed with Elizabeth and came to recognise how meaningful the marriage really was. But not only did Elizabeth bring them together, she sealed her own friendship for life with the old tutor by again going behind Richard's back and organising a poetry reading at the Lunt-Fontanne to raise funds for Philip Burton's new American Musical and Dramatic Academy.

She persuaded celebrities to pay $100 to listen to

herself and Richard recite verse. Richard couldn't get over her audacity and sweetness. He knew she had never appeared on stage and, apart from a rough piece of doggerel, had no memory of the simplest poem.

To prepare for the session, she spent a month practising with Phil Burton, three hours a day, five days a week — just as Richard had worked with him all those years ago in Taibach.

'She knew that many in the audience would come for the ghoulish joy of watching a high wire artist working without a safety net,' said Philip.

During the performance, her Professor Higgins sat behind, mouthing every word she said. But his fears were unfounded.

On the night, Elizabeth was terrified. Again there were the huge crowds outside the theatre when she arrived with her hair piled high and dripping purple flowers. Inside, the fabulous mass of celebrities waited apprehensively for her first stage appearance. They included two sisters of the late President Kennedy, the cast of *Hamlet*, Bea Lillie, Lee Remick, Montgomery Clift, Anita Loos, Walter Wagner and Elizabeth's parents.

Richard began by reading 'To His Coy Mistress' by Andrew Marvell. And marvel of marvels Elizabeth responded in a Cockney accent with Thomas Hardy's 'The Ruined Maid'. She followed up with W.B. Yeats' 'Three Bushes' which told of two women who loved the same man, and came across clearly with the line: 'What could I do but drop down dead if I lost my chastity.'

At this the audience cheered and Bea Lillie whispered: 'If she doesn't get worse soon they'll all be leaving.'

Richard's reading included the 'Death of Kings'

speech from *Richard II*, the St Crispin's Day speech from *Henry V*, and one of his favourite poems, D.H. Lawrence's 'Snake'. Together they read T.S. Eliot's 'Portrait of a Lady' and Psalm 23 — especially moving as Elizabeth spoke in English and Richard took alternate lines in Welsh.

They were given a standing ovation and Richard said, 'I didn't know she was going to be this good. I've never had an ovation like that before.'

'I've never had an ovation, period,' said Elizabeth. 'See, you did get something for your money.'

But the man who benefited most was Philip Burton. He had become director of the acting school in 1962 but the academy was always short of money and was on the point of closing when Elizabeth raised $30,000 from her reading and Richard matched the amount from his own pocket.

Another notable reconciliation took place during *Hamlet*. In his ten-roomed suite at the Regency on Park Avenue, Richard was reunited with Emlyn and Molly Williams. When he answered the door, he kissed them both and whispered that Elizabeth was terrified about the meeting. But there was no need for nervousness.

The last time they had met Emlyn had begged Richard not to leave Sybil for a 'third-rate chorus girl'.

He referred to it by saying: 'You met Mr Hyde then. This time, Mrs Burton, it's Doctor Jekyll.'

'I had been terribly forthright in Rome,' recalls Emlyn. 'But when the years passed by and they really did get married and they were going to be together for life as far as one could see, it was quite rightly all made up. I was appearing in *The Deputy* when Elizabeth telephoned. She was sweet and very nervous, and it was very touching.'

144

As New York paid homage to the Burtons during that summer of supreme success, it was easy to forget how ridiculed and abused they had been only a few months before. Nothing could seriously disturb them after suffering that ordeal. From this point Richard could calculate his fortune in millions. Yet he would never accept that *le scandale* had been chiefly responsible for his sudden elevation. He argued, and at that time Elizabeth didn't contradict him, that his price as an actor did not really soar spectacularly until he had triumphed alone in *Becket, Night of the Iguana* and *Hamlet*.

His isolation was to grow with their retinue. As Professor Coghill expressed it: 'Richard gives me the impression of being protected by secretaries who are themselves protected by other secretaries; and none of them answers letters. A wise provision. Many ancient Emperors were guarded by deaf mutes.' The entourage at this time comprised Burton's two secretaries Jim Benton and George Davis; his personal assistant Bob Wilson — a tall, slim American negro who was his best man at the wedding; Elizabeth's executive factotum Dick Hanley and his assistant John Lee; Gianni Bozzachi, her personal photographer and his wife Claudye who acted as one of her hairdressers. Then came Ron Berkeley, her make-up man; principal chauffeur Gaston Sanz; the tutor Paul Neshamkin; the governess, Bea; and the nurse for baby Maria.

Their regular bodyguard was Bobby LaSalle, an ex-prizefighter who went to Hollywood in 1932, the year Elizabeth was born, as technical adviser on *The Prizefighter and The Lady* starring Maz Baer. It was insane to tangle with him. He wore clip-on bow-ties so that he couldn't be throttled with his own neck-tie, and high-heeled pointed shoes that gave nasty injuries in the wrong places. But for day-to-day protection they relied on Gaston, a short beefy Basque, holder of the Medaille Militaire and the Croix de Guerre for wartime heroics in the Free French Commandos. He wore sinister shades and boasted of a black belt.

The impression this circus made on an outsider is best expressed by Robert Hardy. 'I went to lunch and it was like a minor German court of the seventeenth or eighteenth century, where those admitted were given the most marvellous entertainment — caviar and champagne — and then, at certain times, groups of people were shown the door. This would leave a kind of inner circle and then they were shown the door, leaving a nucleus of three of four. It was marvellous. No one actually came in and bowed, but always one felt the court of servants surrounding him.'

Elizabeth loved the gilded cage and loved love.

It was too exhausting to contemplate as they talked entirely about themselves. Indeed, their words were so widely and solemnly recorded that they might have emanated from the Oracle at Delphi.

From Richard: 'Elizabeth is a combination of a sphinx, a seductress and a woman who holds drawing-room parties for writers. It was not her physical beauty which made me fall in love with her (I'm not going to give you a list of her defects) but her loyalty. What I love in Elizabeth is this: she is an extraordinary mother. She would never sacrifice her children for anything or any man. I feel I now have the last word with Elizabeth. She struggles a bit but it cuts no ice with me. Her tears leave me cold. When she throws a fit of temper I remain like marble. In the end she surrenders unconditionally and lets me make the decisions. For she is a good and generous woman. I have to feel very deeply about someone before I can become emotionally or sexually involved. I've played opposite some ladies who would have welcomed an affair. One, in particular never stopped chasing. But I could hardly bear to touch her. You'd be surprised at the morals of many women stars who are regarded by the public as goody-two-shoes. They leap into bed with any male in grabbing distance. That's what makes me mad when I read stuff hinting that Liz is a scarlet woman because she's been married five times. She's only had five men in her life whereas those goody-two-shoes have lost count.'

Similarly, Elizabeth explained: 'Richard has to be the boss. I know that. It is important for both of us. I need a man strong enough to rule me, and that is not easy. But I think sex is absolutely gorgeous. I'm not a sex queen or a sex symbol. I don't think I want to be one. Maybe Richard and I are sex symbols together because we suggest love. At first, illicit love. It seems curious that our society today finds illicit love more attractive than married love. Our love is married love now. But there is still a suggestion, I suppose, of rampant sex on the wild.'

During their next film *The Sandpiper* Richard had his first short story published — a semi-autobiographical piece about a childhood Christmas in Wales. It was greatly discussed for the possible bearing it might have on his relationship with Elizabeth. For he wrote cryptically: 'When my mother died, she, my sister, had become my mother, and more mother to me than any mother could ever have been. I was immensely proud of her. I shone in the reflection of her green-eyed, black-haired, gipsy beauty. She was innocent and guileless and infinitely protectable. She was naive to the point of saintliness and wept a lot at the misery of others. She felt all tragedies but her own. I had read the Knights of Chivalry and I knew that I had a bounden duty to protect her above all other creatures. It wasn't until thirty years later, when I saw her in another woman, that I realised I had been searching for her all my life.'

Richard laughed at Freudian suggestions and dismissed Sigmund as 'dirty minded old Fraud'. It may not have been an Oedipus complex — the unconscious sexual love of a son for his mother, plus a jealous hatred for his father. Daddy Ni, his natural father was feckless, yet Richard loved him. But his sister Cissie was his surrogate mother, and Richard hated her husband.

Elizabeth certainly mothered Richard, and outside the bedroom treated him as a Jewish or Irish son. If he drank, she made sure he ate. And when he ate she made sure he ate up his greens. Her own dress sense was slightly tarty, but his was eccentric, due no doubt to his complete inability to distinguish one colour from another. For Christmas she bought him thirty-seven tailor-made suits at a cost of £5,000, but during the making of *The Spy Who Came In From The Cold* he exasperated her by wearing a crumpled, ill-fitting, twelve guinea suit and a shabby raincoat that was the wardrobe of Alec Leamas, the seedy, shiftless, secret agent of John Le Carre's best selling novel. Instead of taking it off after filming he would wear it around Dublin pubs.

For two months they occupied the penthouse suite in the Gresham Hotel, and it was an uneasy time for both of them. Elizabeth had some £20,000 worth of jewels stolen. Daughter Maria went down with measles and Richard, now in his fortieth year, in keeping with the miserable Leamas, not only kept on his suit but kept on his character. He drank too much. He described how 'I had to knock back a large whisky. It was the last shot of the day and I decided to use the real stuff, the hard stuff. We did forty-seven takes. Imagine it, love, forty-seven whiskies.'

But it was Elizabeth, though not working, who faced the greatest strain. In February she flew to Paris to console her chauffeur, Gaston, whose sixteen-year-old son had been killed in a shooting gallery accident. She shared in his grief, accompanying him to the inquest and the funeral. 'Only her compassion and support,' he said, 'saved me from myself. I wouldn't be here now if it wasn't for her.'

Elizabeth had been only a few days back in Dublin when she had to fly off again following the news that her father had suffered a stroke in Los Angeles. For days, as he hovered between life and death, she held the family together. Mr Taylor survived. And the words of Richard's 'Christmas Story' came back to mind: 'she felt all the tragedies, except her own ...'

The Spy Who Came In From The Cold faithfully followed the book except in one trivial detail: the name of Leamas' girlfriend, played by Claire Bloom, had been changed from Liz to Nan.

Not that Elizabeth cared one way or another. She told me: 'She was as sweet as a razor. I met her once in a powder room when she was peeling off her eyelashes. And I said to her: 'Oh, do you wear false eyelashes? Aren't they marvellous? They are so terribly clever. I've never seen any before. May I look at them please?" And I sort of put one up to my own eyelashes and said, "My God, how ever can you stand to wear them? Aren't they terribly heavy? Oh, but they do make one look terribly glamorous. I look like Sophia Loren. It's terrific, isn't it? But I don't think I could wear them. Don't they make your eyes feel impossibly heavy? I mean to have to wear them all the time ..."'

For this saccharine dialogue with her husband's ex-mistress, Elizabeth assumed a little girl voice of sufficient high-pitched innocence to make sleeping dogs cock up their ears and begin to whimper in distress.

'It is my favourite scene,' said Richard.

The scenes that were to follow in *Who's Afraid of Virginia Woolf?* were not.

The shooting scheduled for two months in 1965 dragged on from July to December and gradually the characters took over the actors. Elizabeth played Martha — a fat, profanely vicious bitch, married to George, a mediocre college professor. The other couple was played by George Segal as the ambitious young biologist and Sandy Dennis as his whispering wife.

Before the first expletive hit director Mike Nichols, telegrams arrived from Shelley Winters and many others familiar with the play — messages begging them not to do it. 'No marriage can withstand the corrosive hatred of those lines ... You'll end up fighting like cat and dog at home after doing it day after day on set.'

Producer Ernest Lehman said that Burton was always protesting that the man he was playing was not him. 'The one day I saw him in costume as George, I was bowled over. "By God Richard, you are George. You really are." And he replied, "Of course I am, Ernie. Didn't you know that? I am George. George is me."'

Chapter Eleven

RECENTLY, WHILST AWASH with booze and abed with a nymphomaniac scribe, Richard, in the middle of some intimate soliloquy, broke off and said: 'I can do whatever I like without anyone asking me what I am doing and why I am doing it. I actually believe in the marriage vows, but I cheated on Elizabeth after her fortieth birthday party. I found myself looking at younger women. Then I suddenly realised I was bored with Elizabeth.'

He had definitely cheated on her after her fortieth birthday and had certainly started searching for what Sybil called 'reassurance' after his own fortieth birthday.

At first he found it in extravagance. To excuse it to me he quoted Victor Hugo. 'I wish for the superfluous, for the useless, for the extravagant, for the too much, for that which is not going for anything.' At the time we were sitting aboard the *Beatriz of Bolivia*, a 200-ton diesel yacht he had hired from the Patino tin family at the modest rental of £1,000 a week, and which was now parked alongside the Tower of London in the Thames.

'But why?' I said. Richard pointed to the mess of stains on the Wilton carpet. 'That's why. That's cat and dog shit. Elizabeth wouldn't come without her pets and the *Kalizma* is in dry-dock.'

Guides on the river pleasure boats gave the Beefeaters earache with their 'on the left ladies and gentlemen, we have the Burton's yacht — the most expensive floating dog kennel in the world.'

And so it was.

This new image of the Burtons as super-spenders was launched with the purchase of *Kalizma*, renamed after Kate, Liza and little Maria. Richard casually bought it when they had chartered her in the South of France and Elizabeth fell in love with the romantic story behind a yacht that had been built to house an enormous organ so that the eccentric owner could take her out in heavy storms to get the right atmosphere for playing Bach.

The first thing they ripped out in a £100,000 face-lift was the organ.

'He gave me fabulous gifts and all the world knew about them,' Elizabeth was to say later. 'But he also gave me other gifts for no apparent reason and asked me not to tell the press about them. And while he was giving me those gifts he looked at me in a certain way, as if he had to beg my pardon for something he didn't tell me.'

Richard bought her the 33-carat Krupp diamond for $305,000 — her 'ping pong perfect gem' which she had won by taking ten points off him at table-tennis. 'I was pissed at the time,' said Burton. The Krupp diamond was followed by the $37,000 La Peregrina pearl, which King Philip of Spain gave to Henry VIII's daughter, Mary Tudor and so on through to the 69.42 carat Cartier diamond at a mere million-odd dollars.

The latter piece of ice went on display in New York and brought editorial anger from the *New York Times*: 'The peasants have been lining up outside

Cartier's this week to gawk at a diamond as big as the Ritz that costs well over a million dollars. It is destined to hang around the neck of Mrs Richard Burton. As somebody said, it would have been nice to wear in the tumbril on the way to the guillotine.

'Actually, the inch-long, inch-thick Cartier diamond is a smart buy because it goes with everything. It won't clash with the smaller Krupp diamond already given by Mr Burton as a modest gift to his wife. It won't seem out of place on the yacht parked in the Bahamas or the Mediterranean where Beautiful People spend much of their time, not to mention money, impressing each other.

'In this age of vulgarity marked by such minor matters as war and poverty, it gets harder every day to scale the heights of true vulgarity. But given some loose millions, it can be done — and worse, admired.'

But vulgarity is admired, and worse still from the point of view of peasants, by royalty. When Princess Margaret saw Elizabeth's Krupp diamond at a wedding reception she said: 'That's the most vulgar thing I've ever seen.'

'Want to try it on?' said Elizabeth.

'Oh, yes please,' replied Margaret.

There were other shows of vulgar ostentation like a one million dollar, ten-passenger twin jet and the paintings. One day in their Hampstead house Elizabeth showed me the collection — unprotected on the walls. 'Now I've given Richard the Van Gogh and the Monet. And see that Utrillo? It's a painting of the Château de Chillon by Lake Geneva where Richard and I used to meet after *Cleopatra*. We managed to pick it up at an auction. And that little one there, that's a Noel Coward. Yes the one between the Degas and the Modigliani.'

She showed them with pleasure, with the same delight one gets from showing off the family album. In the corner of one of the bedrooms more framed paintings and sketches were piled on the floor. Elizabeth sorted them out, tossing aside an Andy Warhol. 'Now here we have our own work — that's one by Liza, this one by Michael and here's an original Elizabeth Burton.'

They had accumulated the 'display' since *Who's Afraid of Virginia Woolf?* — with *The Taming of the Shrew, The Comedians, Boom!* as co-stars. Elizabeth had played opposite Marlon Brando in *Reflections in a Golden Eye*, Robert Mitcham, in *Secret Ceremony*, Warren Beatty in *The Only Game in Town*, and Michael Caine in *Zee & Co*. Richard had clocked up one more than this total with *Where Eagles Dare, Staircase, Anne of The Thousand Days, Raid on Rommel* and *Villain*.

On the day Elizabeth showed me around the gallery he said: 'Not too bad, old love not too bad. One year we get something extraordinary like four million pounds, non taxable. I don't know exactly what I'm worth. Thirty million perhaps (whether it was dollars or pounds he never said). I don't really know. When I went from the Air Force into the theatre my ambition was to make a million, but after I made it I felt the need to make two million, then three and then four. And then I found to my surprise that money is not all that interesting. It's only important if you haven't got any. Otherwise it's just monopoly money. We went over to diamonds when gold began wobbling. We reckoned they were as good a bet as any.'

Some say the display of wealth started when he was making *Anne of The Thousand Days* with an unknown actress by the name of Genevieve Bujold whose youthful beauty not only captivated Richard but put paid to Elizabeth's ambition of playing Anne Boleyn to Richard's Henry VIII.

There could be some truth in this. She had been toppled from the Top Ten Box Office Stars and was lacerated by Rex Reed after *Secret Ceremony:* 'The disintegration of Elizabeth Taylor has been a very sad thing to stand by helplessly and watch, but something ghastly has happened over the course of her last four or five films. She has become a hideous parody of herself — a fat, sloppy, yelling, screeching banshee.'

But more likely they were stacking their wealth up for a rainy day. And when the storm did break it was devastating.

It was American Independence Day, the fourth of July, 1973. And Elizabeth Taylor had a written declaration of independence all of her own; one that grabbed the headlines and aroused more immediate comment than did Thomas Jefferson when 197 years previously he penned the 'causes which impel separation'.

From her suite in New York's Regency Hotel she wrote: 'I am convinced that it would be a good and constructive idea if Richard and I separated for a while. Maybe we loved each other too much — not that I ever believed such a thing was possible. But we have been in each other's pockets constantly, never being apart except for matters of life and death, and I believe it has caused a temporary breakdown of communication.

'I believe with all my heart that the separation will ultimately bring us back to where we should be — and that is together. I think in a few days time I shall return to California, because my mother is there and I have many old and true friends out there as well. And friends are to help each other, aren't they? Isn't that what it's all supposed to be about? And if anyone reads anything lascivious into this statement, all I can say is it must be in the mind of the reader — not in mine or my friends, or my husband. Wish us well please during this most difficult time.'

This declaration could not have been given more publicity had it been signed 'Elizabeth R' instead of Elizabeth Taylor Burton.

It is unusual when a wife runs home to her mother for her to write a letter to the world.

What was even more extraordinary was that next day the world's press dutifully published this message in full and commented upon it as if it were a royal proclamation.

In Britain it occupied the whole of the *Daily Mirror's* front page and a page-one editorial commented: 'It was obvious that an explosive package-deal like the Burton marriage must eventually assault itself to a standstill. It was love in a minefield, about as tranquil as a bad gear change by a ten-ton lorry. Whether the marriage has sunk, or merely struck a reef, awaits some word from Mr Burton.'

The word was not long in coming. Burton held court for the press at the house of his lawyer, Aaron Frosch, at Quogue, Long Island. He treated them like critics rather than journalists and gave them a breakfast performance armed with that all too familiar prop — a glass of vodka. It was as if he were auditioning for the role of the most misunderstood husband on the block.

To the amazement of the hard-nosed hacks he gave them the gravedigger's scene from Hamlet: 'Here hung those lips that I have kissed I know not how soft. Where be your gibes now? your gambols? your songs?

your flashes of merriment that were wont to set the table on a roar ... Now get you to my lady's chamber, and tell her, let her paint an inch thick, to this favour she must come; make her laugh at that.'

Burton was acting up to his own towering style — and he knew it. Alas! Poor Richard had to face up to the slings and arrows of his outrageous fortune. Reporters fired the questions. He finished the remains of the vodka bottle, belched, and said:

'Perhaps my indifference to Elizabeth's personal problems triggered off this situation. She has been very worried about her mother who is pretty ill. Maybe it is something else. Women are strange creatures. I don't know what it is or what she's really talking about. As far as I know there isn't a separation. But it only takes one to make a separation.

'I do not believe there is anyone else in Elizabeth's life. She is a splendid child and I am very fond of the lady. But who knows what goes on in the secret feminine mind. I haven't spoken to her since her extraordinary statement. The frightful thing is I am amused by all this — disturbed too, naturally. I find the situation wildly fascinating.'

So did millions of others. Elizabeth and Richard, it seemed, were spoiled children demanding total attention, and with such relenting force they were getting it.

What had happened? What explosive situation had occurred to tear apart so suddenly the most intimately publicised lovers in modern history?

I drop the questions into this chapter as they were posed then. For everyone was taken by surprise.

The simple answer was that it wasn't really sudden and no single happening was totally responsible. To understand the mounting pressures that made their love so fragile one needs to go back a year, to the summer of '72.

Firstly, there came a very minor family disturbance. While they were celebrating Liz's fortieth birthday in Budapest her son, nineteen-year-old Michael, and his bride of eighteen months moved out of the £30,000 Hampstead home that had been given to them as a wedding present and set up a family commune in the Welsh Cambrian Mountains. Michael, like his younger brother Christopher, was a drop-out from Millfield, the most expensive public school in England, and his problems mounted. His young wife walked out with the baby, his den mother Jo was in the family way and he was fined £100 for smoking pot.

All this had nothing to do with Richard. Just before the birthday celebrations he was jolted off the wagon when he was told that his brother Ivor had died. He displayed complete indifference to the world's most glamorous grandmother clucking over her chicks. But she, in turn, was far from indifferent to the interest he was showing in the chicks who were playing intimate scenes with him in the film *Bluebeard*.

'If anyone had reason to be jealous over that film it was me,' she said. 'There was someone who put too much passion in certain scenes. And moreover she was naked. I smacked her face for her pains, and Richard. I don't know how many plates I broke over his head.'

The naked lady in question was Dora Zakablukowa. The other women in the film were Raquel Welch, Joey Heatherton, Nathalie Delon and Virni Lisi. 'What I couldn't stomach,' sniffed Elizabeth, 'was that he seemed to like the excessive show of passion.' She took her revenge by flying to

158

Rome and going out to dinner with Aristotle Onassis. But Richard didn't even notice. She phoned him at five in the morning and screamed: 'Get that woman out of my bed.'

When Richard asked the director Edward Dmytryk how Elizabeth knew he had an actress in bed, Eddie said: 'You must be joking. You're surrounded by her agents.'

Matters didn't improve with their final, and ill-starred movie together — aptly entitled *Divorce His, Divorce Hers*. In a devastating account of what went on behind the scenes, actress Carrie Nye told *Time* magazine: 'After a spell, it became apparent that Mr Burton did not do an awful lot of work after lunch and Mrs Taylor-Burton did not arrive until about quarter-to-three in the afternoon. What was actually eaten, if anything, at these cosy lunches for twelve (most of whom are in the Burton's permanent employ, as opposed to us temporary help) is lost to memory. What was imbibed will be permanently inscribed on my liver for the rest of my days ... Mr Burton could generally be relied upon to knock off work early, usually with a magnificent display of temper, foot stamping, and a few exit lines delivered in the finest St Crispin's Day style. My favourite was "I am old and grey and incredibly gifted."'

And so, after nine years of marriage ('and three clandestine years', as Burton so delicately phrases it) they came to Miss Taylor's Declaration of Independence.

Richard went into a clinic to dry out and get into shape to star with Sophia Loren in Rome. Elizabeth found comfort with old friends and new in Hollywood. Suddenly it was as if they had donned the stage make-up of that masochistic pair they played in Virginia

Woolf and were using the media as a psychiatrist's babble-bench to pour out the most intimate details of their marriage.

He: 'Peter Lawford has come between us. What Elizabeth sees in him is a mystery. But he of all people has driven us apart. Elizabeth in the past has made a fool of herself with various actors. She got a thrashing for it. But like a spoiled child she enjoys undermining me. One gets tired of it. A man must have some peace. The problem is that Elizabeth and I have grown apart intellectually. I have only twenty-four hours a day. I read, write and film. Elizabeth is constantly seeking problems of one kind or another. She worries about her figure, about her family, about the colour of her teeth. She expects that I drop everything to devote myself to these problems. I cannot.'

She: 'There were several woman and they weren't the ugliest. At first it amused me. But there comes a point when you shouldn't overdo anything. I am a jealous woman and, finally, the smallest glance or the smallest smile would cause me to come apart inside. I could no longer bear being deceived. We quarrelled, regardless whether someone was present or not. Our quarrelling finally destroyed our love. I am very quarrelsome. I always wanted to be in the centre and loved being desired by men. That gave me the feeling of being even more beautiful. Richard couldn't stand it. He had a murderous jealousy and because of this we several times hit each other. Maybe I've been wrong not to take greater care of my figure. He always told me it wasn't important if I was a little stout and I always believed him. I am not so sure now.'

Richard called his co-star in Italy and asked if he might stay with her and her husband, Carlo Ponti, at their villa in Marino. On 13 July he moved in. A week

160

later he was at Rome's Ciampino airport with representatives of the world press following an announcement from Los Angeles that Elizabeth was flying in to kiss and make up. But if the cameramen and reporters packing the tiny airport expected to see the repentant husband running out to meet the plane they were mistaken. He sat hunched in the back of his green Rolls as Elizabeth's private jet taxied to a standstill fifty yards away. For twenty minutes he stayed there. She was wearing blue jeans, an orange T-shirt and her 69.42 carat ring. And it was she who had to run the gauntlet before being bundled into the back of the car by security men. They kissed and Elizabeth and the chauffeur were weeping as they headed for the Ponti villa.

Within days the rumours were running riot again and soon the *paparazzi* were stealing spectacular peeping shots of Elizabeth being comforted in the arms of Sophia upstairs while Burton glowered out of the window below. Elizabeth moved out. The reconciliation had lasted exactly nine days.

Suddenly a third man turned up in the headlines. Henry Weinberg. 'Henry who?' asked Burton and the gossip columnists echoed his amazement. They had been introduced by a mutual friend in Hollywood. Two days later Henry had the suite next to Elizabeth at Rome's Grand Hotel and was accompanying her to the studios where she was making *Identikit*.

Henry's arrival on the scene certainly shook Burton's long held belief that Elizabeth didn't play around. But within twenty-four hours, and days before the gossip columnists, he had a full biography of the man who was sharing his wife's bed. Henry was born in Holland, started work as a luggage boy at Amsterdam's Krasnapolsky Hotel, emigrated to

America as a waiter, prospered as a second-hand ca
salesman, fiddled speedometers, was caught, and wa
now in property in Los Angeles. He had first me
Elizabeth at the Candy night club in Beverly Hills
The man who introduced them was Peter Lawford.

Elizabeth traipsed around the world with Henr
showing him off and saying she was 'in good Dutc
hands'. Burton it seems was in the good Italian arms o
Sophia. They had spent weekends together on th
Kalizma and Richard had written in the *Ladies' Hom
Journal*: 'I adore her. She me. Platonically, of course

In November, immediately after returning t
California with Henry, Elizabeth went into th
Scripps Institute Clinic. She had been sufferin
stomach cramps. She was frightened. No superstar
indeed very few women, had collected so many scar
— tracheotomy, hysterectomy, three Caesarians, plu
three spinal operations involving bone grafts fror
pelvis and hip. And now she was haunted by the mos
alarming possibility of all: that she might have
malignant cancerous growth. She was operated o
and a cyst was removed from her right ovary. Sh
telephoned Richard.

Burton who had spent six months making the bes
of freedom was pleased to hear her voice. 'I had tol
her to go. "Get out," I said. And to my astonishmen
she went. Time went by, months of torture, agony
and then, the telephone rings. And there is thi
strange woman, very strong, very odd, very perverse
very curious, who says, "Can I come back home?" o
something like that. And I said, "Oh sure"'.

He responded immediately, positively, unhesitatingly
He jetted into Los Angeles aboard a chartere
Mystere executive jet. He told the staff. 'I'm th
husband. I'm tired and I want the bed next to m

162

wife.' And when he moved in, Henry moved out.

It was an emotion-charged climatic scene.

They flew to Italy and she accompanied him back to Orville, California where he began work with Lee Marvin in *The Klansman*. He also started drinking more heavily than ever. Just a few weeks after he had 'honked' Elizabeth's breasts at Sophia Loren's villa 'just to show that Rich and Liz are back together again', he was honking other breasts. He gave an eighteen-year-old pancake waitress a £200 ring and boasted of his other conquests. Even Lee Marvin wasn't amused. Elizabeth flew back into the arms of Henry.

Burton was in a darkened room in Santa Monica Hospital suffering from suspected cirrhosis of the liver and undergoing detoxification, when his wife delivered another Elizabethan proclamation — announcing with deep regret that the reconciliation had failed and the marriage had died of irreconcilable differences.

Richard groaned: 'Surely propinquity must breed some kind of durable affection, even only for the weaknesses.'

The only propinquinity that Elizabeth was feeling was in her nearness to Henry. 'I know I'm a pretty controversial woman. I know some people, whom I've never met, loathe me as a Wicked Woman. Well let them. If they want to hate me as a *femme fatale* good luck to them. Better they hate me than their children or their husbands.'

It would have been easier for a scriptwriter to light a penny candle from a star than to write a scenario for such rich stuff. But that wasn't the half of it.

Following their divorce in June 1974 Richard took up with a string of women including the coloured actress Jean Bell and Princess Elizabeth of Yugoslavia. The latter was Elizabeth's best friend and when Richard announced his engagement to her she was furious until she read that the second Elizabeth had walked out after finding Richard coupled with the former.

In between times he went into two films: a remake of Brief Encounter with Sophia Loren playing the Celia Johnson role. Robert Shaw was going to play the Trevor Howard part, but could not be released from Jaws and Richard stepped in. It was a chance to visit England and renew acquaintance with Sophia.

From Brief Encounter, which went unnoticed, he went nervously into Walk With Destiny to play Churchill. But it was what he said about Churchill in articles for The Times and America's TV Guide rather than his performance, that caused an uproar. Everyone, especially those who had listened to his stories about meeting Churchill when he was playing Hamlet at the Old Vic, presumed he was a great admirer of Winston. The Times ran his article under the heading 'To play Churchill is to hate him.' And he made no bones about it. Richard described him as a 'monster' and a 'vindictive toy-soldier child'. Not content with that he said that in playing Churchill he 'realised afresh that I hate Churchill and all his kind. I hate them virulently. They have stalked down the corridors of endless power all through history.' To cap it all he blamed Churchill for the bombing of Dresden and said that he was a coward. He also compared him to Attila the Hun, Hitler and Stalin.

Churchill's family were as deeply offended as the rest of the establishment. The Times itself said 'Burton is now more clearly seen for what he is: an actor of talent, though not a great one — and a fool.'

Richard showed a cheerful indifference. To reporters he shrugged his shoulders 'Attila, Hitler, Churchill — they were all killers.'

There were letters from generals and clergymen, but the public didn't care. Elizabeth had written an intimate letter to Richard (published of course): 'I know we will be together in every biblical sense for ever so why are we afraid of that legal bit of paper ... someday, somewhere, you son of a bitch, something will make you realise that you can't live without me.'

And so it came to pass.

In October 1976 they were in each others arms on the banks of the Chobe River in Botswana, and Elizabeth penned her own wedding report. The world gobbled it up with delight. Richard had again answered the call. He took her to Africa. She wrote: 'Beneath God's skies we repeated our vows. Baboons danced up and down, fishes were our bridesmaids, hippopotumuses were our witnesses and a rhino stood guard. We were back where we belonged. I thought I had Big C. I gave Richard a Valium. He whispered poetry. We kissed. We are stuck together like chickens to tar for lovely always.'

The greatest love story in the world had become the World of Walt Disney. 'Lovely always' didn't last the year. The chickens came unstuck.

Looking back Richard says about his second wedding: 'Don't ask me. It was like a huge dream. I remember thinking: What am I doing here? Odd place to be married in the bush by an African gentleman. It was very curious. An extraordinary adventure doomed from the start, of course.'

The ex-ex-Mrs Burton went back to another lover, a Maltese Lothario Peter Darmanin. He seemed to love her. He was quoted as saying:

165

'Our affair lasted seven weeks. But it was like seven months — no seven years — because we were with each other every moment. That is the only way you can be with Elizabeth. She needs that kind of loving. She is passionate in bed and I must admit that I did not sleep much during those seven weeks.'

Little did Richard know it, but another adventure was starting — and that too was doomed from the start.

He was on the ski slopes with Emlyn William's son, Brook, when he spotted a tall, gorgeous blonde. 'I turned around and there was this beautiful creature nine feet tall. Absolutely startling. She could stop a stampede. I kept wondering when she was going to appear again. I couldn't wait. "Get her up to the house," I kept saying. Brook knew her a little and my luck was in. She started coming up to the house — two, three, four times a week.'

This blonde, five feet ten and twenty-seven years old, was Susan Hunt, the former fashion model separated from racing driver James Hunt.

Six months later, in the summer of 1976, they were married. 'Marriage is the right thing for us to do,' said Richard. 'I plan on it lasting forever.'

Then on 4 December 1976, Elizabeth wed John W. Warner, the US Senator from Capitol Hill. 'I've never been so happy,' she said with tears in her eyes. 'I'm really so much in love with John. I don't think I have ever really felt this good and lucky.'

Let *Time* magazine write the postscript. Back in 1963 they had written: 'Show a Welshman like Burton one thousand exits, one of which is marked *self-destruction* and he will go right through that door. The outcome of the Taylor-Burton game must inevitably yield up a loser. If he should ever marry her, he will be the Oxford boy who became the fifth husband of the Wife of Bath. If she loses him, she loses her reputation as a fatal beauty, an all-consuming man-eater, the Cleopatra of the twentieth century.'

On 15 March 1982 *Time* reported:

'"*Rwyn dy garu di*" (I love you, in Welsh) proclaimed Elizabeth Taylor, fifty, arms outstretched, as she swept across the stage of London's Duke of York's Theatre towards her two-time former husband Richard Burton, fifty-six. Burton who was giving a reading from Dylan Thomas, cooed back: 'Say it again my petal. Say it again.' The lady complied, and lo, with all the eye-rolling gaucherie of a Groucho Marx–Margaret Dumont coupling, Liz and Dick were, gasp, together again. She was in London for the West End run of her Broadway hit *The Little Foxes*. At a lavish fiftieth birthday party thrown in her honour at a Mayfair nightclub, the pair toasted each other with champagne and by evening's end were dancing cheek to cheek. Taylor and Senator John Warner separated in December 1981, and Burton and his wife Susan also parted. But the seven-time-married Taylor and the four-time-married Burton scotched notions that another wedding might be in the offing. Said Burton: 'We love each other with a passion so furious that we burn each other out.'

Burton was to explain that passion later: 'I took her home. I was upset to find the place infested by her entourage of hangers-on and homosexuals. I ordered them out of the room. Then Elizabeth looked at me and said: "Hey buster, you're thin. Aren't you going to joss me?" I just took her in my arms and kissed her. I pulled her down on the couch — just like that. Then and there. For old times' sake.'

Chapter Twelve

THE REASON FOR biography is to answer the question: What's he like? Ah, that's the rub. What is he like or what was he like? The spirit is the true self, the self the ego and the impediment to the recognition of Richard Burton lies within himself. If he is difficult to please, it is because he is rarely pleased with himself. As with all men, one can only look at the husk and guess at the nut. And what one really sees and feels in Burton is charm — a charm that is wrapped in humour that in itself becomes disarming to those who mistrust charming people as being spoiled.

Nature, by some extraordinary shake of the genetical dice, gave Burton the sort of looks that are attractive to young romantic girls, aesthetic bachelors and women who respond to the sexual embrace of the face. Age has not withered that quality which inspired everyone around him to accept him as some startling creature blessed with a charisma that he himself has never used to the disadvantage of others, except perhaps Eddie Fisher.

When still in his teens and courting the girls, Richard — unlike John Huston's old dad Walter — never played at the waiting game, never gave the world time to take a couple of whirls, but instead let it come his way.

Listen! He is sixteen, his school companions, now schoolmasters are speaking. Dennis Burgess: 'He had this extraordinary adult attitude, this maturity and almost worldly sophistication that made him different from the other boys. He used to say, "What is it? Is it something we've got? Or is it something they lack."'

Gerry 'Luther' Lewis: 'He was university material all right. Brilliant. A normal person who had academic ability and the right potential would have to swot hard, but he could do it without seeming to do anything other than drink and play rugby.'

Listen! Now he is eighteen and Nevill Coghill, Merton professor of English literature, Oxford is speaking: 'I wrote in 1944. "This boy is a genius and will be a great actor. He is outstandingly handsome and robust and very masculine and with deep inward fire." More than thirty years later I haven't changed my mind. I have had many students of very great gifts and many of very little. But I have had only two men of genius to teach — W.H. Auden and Richard Burton. When they happen one cannot mistake them.'

Hark to Robert Hardy, the Shakespearean and TV actor who played Churchill, the war leader who addressed Burton as 'My Lord Hamlet' and whom Burton was later to identify as a 'vindictive, toy-soldier child'. Says Hardy: 'Richard was a genius in the effortless way he attracted everybody — the most attractive creature I have ever come across. It was the size of his personality that made me think of him as a great man. Everything in him was larger than life. Fine athlete, brilliant talker, superb drinker, everything. To us at Oxford he was a natural born prince. The fact that he hadn't any money and didn't come from a palace made no difference. I remember having a long conversation about morality, about what is right and what is wrong. And he said to me: "We are the myth-makers". In any generation and in any system of life there are myth-makers. Richard had to become a myth from the moment he was born. Whatever he did he was destined to do greatly. He did become a myth. When he told me "We are the myth-makers," he meant: "I am a myth-maker". And he was right.'

Genius. Myth-maker. It sounds too exaggerated. It is said that the world more often rewards the appearance of merit than merit itself. And this could be true. He is a fantast. His principal aim is to entertain, rarely to inform. Years ago after working with him in *The Robe,* Dawn Adams observed, 'Richard is a remarkable actor on the stage and film. But in private life he is even a better one. When you are with him, you believe him, but afterwards, you wonder.'

Dennis Burgess says, 'There is that terrible phrase someone employed — "legitimate hyperbole". This is Rich. I used to say to him. "That's not the story you told six weeks ago". So often he contradicts himself and it's impossible to pin him down to hard facts. Sometimes his stories are out and out lies.'

On the David Frost show, for example, his longest and funniest and most elaborate anecdote recalled the time he was playing Prince Hal at Stratford and how he had drunk steadily through St David's Day before going on stage in chain-mail and armour. Eloquently and discreetly he described his cross-legged agony during a play lasting three and a quarter hours — 'with a vein standing out on my forehead, and just hoping and waiting for the curtain to come down' — and how the floodgates finally burst open and how in his discomforture he went after Redgrave so ferociously that he snapped a sword in half and threw Sir Michael across the stage. In fact the St David's Day angle, of which he had made such play, was entirely false since the production did not open until a month after the day of the patron saint of Wales. But in essence his 'once more into the breeches' story was true.

Stanley Baker told me that Burton actually 'pinched' stories about his own father, a one-legged coal miner in the Rhondda Valley. 'My father had a job as a night-watchman in Tylerstown. He adored kids and when they gathered around his fire he used to frighten the life out of them by saying he could hypnotise them. "Just look into my eyes for three seconds," he would say, "and you'll be out like a light." And they would all hide their eyes or look away. He was also the chairman for concerts in the main pub, and whenever a fight broke he would be up there on the window sill swinging his crutches. Anyway, when Richard and I were in Anzio together, I heard him telling these stories to an American journalist. And I said, "Eh, hold on a second. That's my father you're talking about."'

Burton readily admits he is often putting on an act. 'I suppose most actors never really stop talking, never stop acting. After all, what is life if not one long desperate struggle to hold the centre of the stage? Certainly, I like to be the centre of attention, to dominate conversations if I can.' Philip Burton has recalled that Richard even in schooldays, had this compulsive urge to keep on acting, whether off stage or on: 'The most outstanding thing was, quite simply, that he never, ever, bored me.'

Hardy says the same thing. 'Forget the film star bit. He has this tremendous physical presence which fills a room. And he always had it. When you meet Richard, you meet a great man who just happens to have become an actor.'

Donald Huston has no hesitation in saying: 'Richard has one of the best brains I have ever encountered. He is a mass of facts and information and knowledge, and with his gifts and brains he could have been just as famous in any field he had chosen to take up. If he had taken up politics for instance, I would have expected him to end up as Prime Minister.'

Paul Daneman: 'He is one of nature's leaders, one of those people who — whatever he did in life — would have got to the top. In a way, I rather suspect that he may have secretly regretted becoming an actor because it is not a profession to keep one's intellectual powers at full stretch.'

John Neville: 'Richard has one of the best minds in an actor that I've ever met — a brilliant, extraordinary mind. We would be up all night drinking after alternating as Iago and Othello. One morning at rehearsals I was shattered and he said: "I read the most marvellous book last night after I left you." I said, "Oh, yes, what was that?" He replied, "*The History of Mathematics*." Well, apart from the title, I thought when the hell did he get the time to read it. But he really did you see.'

Emlyn Williams: 'Richard is tremendously cultivated; much more than I am really, because he knows poems and books by heart — the kind of works which one thinks one knows but doesn't really. In the end you believe you've read them. But Richard really has. He is incredibly well read. And yet he makes light of it all. He is so unpretentious; in himself he is a completely real person. He has a great talent as a writer. He rarely writes letters, but when my book *George* was published, he sent me the most marvellous letter from Rome. I could tell then that he was longing to write, and indeed he said: "I do hope that one day I shall be able to do the same sort of thing." The ability is very much there.'

His considerable potential as a writer was first revealed with the publication of his Welsh 'Christmas Story', the reviews of which delighted him more than the notices he received for his first *Hamlet*. Since then he has contributed articles to many leading American magazines. Mostly pieces too lightweight in subject matter to stretch him fully, but all prepared with meticulous scholarship. He really cares what the critics think of his writing. He will go over an essay again and again, reluctant to let it go lest there be one loose word, one unbalanced phrase, one hint of a cliché that has escaped his attention. No other activity does he tackle with such grim seriousness and painstaking attention to detail. As he puts it: 'The only thing in life is language. Speaking other men's words is an adolescent craft. Let's face it, I have not been a dedicated actor. It's all bloody marvellous luck. I had the right sort of clock and the right sort of coal-black bobbing Welsh voice. I also had the amazing luck of being adopted by Phil Burton and going to Oxford and other places away from my large Jenkins family. Olivier, Gielgud, Scofield, Richardson. They love acting. Me, I'm different. Much of the time it's just tedium for me. Actors? They're poor, abject creatures. They must have the centre of the stage or at least the second centre. They'd like to stop but they can't. And of that august company of idiots, I'm afraid I'm a member.

'What I'd like to do now is appear in two plays: Jean

Paul Sartre's *The Devil and the Good God* and *King Lear* — and then just disappear from view.'

Warren Mitchell sighs: 'He always says it. One hopes, one thinks that he must play Lear. But I don't think he'd have the stamina now. He'd have to go back into training for that. I agree that he could have been anything he wanted. But he sees himself in this tragic role. He has this self destructive thing. Because there is no doubt there were once two up and coming giants — Scofield and Burton. They were the same age. They were friends. And there was no doubt that the theatre was in their hands. Like it was with Olivier and Gielgud, say. And Burton has disappointed me. But then, I should talk of dedication. We've all sold out some way or other. I swore I'd never do a television commercial, but eventually the price was so good I couldn't refuse. I like the comforts of life too.'

Has Burton sold out?

Well, unlike Mitchell, and Olivier for that matter, he has never appeared in a commercial on the Idiot Box and has never accepted anything less than top billing on stage and screen since 1951.

It may have been a case of *never mind the quality, feel the quantity*, but rather like Orson Welles, another cursed with the misfortune of having started at the top, he will always be pursued by nit-picking critics and flea-bitten showbusiness philosophers who, collectively, have not sufficient wit to clog the foot of a gnat. Their careless invention of tired aphorisms like 'flawed genius' and 'his own worst enemy' can be applied to all popular heroes of the media. But did Richard Burton ever sell himself as cheaply as his critics did? I think not.

He may have deserted the English stage, but not the theatre. During his Elizabethan phase he did a record-breaking *Hamlet* on Broadway and in 1976, when he recovered from the horrors of *The Klansman*, he returned to play Dysart the psychiatrist in Equus. Walter Kerr in *The New York Times* said it was 'the best work in his life'. Clive Barnes called him 'the most promising middle-aged, English-speaking actor now alive'. Four years later he was back on stage in a revival of *Camelot*. His King Arthur was twenty years older than his original, but critics throughout a half a dozen cities across America, including New York, thought it a better portrayal. Before the tour ended he was taken ill and underwent an operation to relieve a chronic spinal condition.

He married Susan Hunt in 1976 and paid tribute to her on the Dick Cavett TV show: 'It was the first time I had been on stage without a drink and I have never been so bloody scared in all my life. Without her I might very easily be dead. The audiences were fantastically kind, and they gave me standing ovations and all that, but every night we never knew if I'd crack.'

Many thought he had when he was taken ill during one performance of *Camelot* in July 1980. Nobody believed the explanation of 'nausea and exhaustion' and it wasn't until the following April when he was operated on that critics realised that Burton had played the whole run with nightly doses of pain killing drugs.

In between marriages with Elizabeth Taylor, Burton went into a film called *Jackpot* in February 1975. But despite his name and fame it ran out of money and was never completed. During his next film *Exorcist II: The Heretic* in the following year he married Susan Hunt, but unfortunately the film didn't run out of money and *was* made. The critics slammed it as one of the worst films ever, and even the director John Boorman admitted that cinema managers were afraid to wear their tuxedos in case they were lynched. Richard said, 'Everybody was right. I was wrong. I would come home and read the stupid lines aloud and Susan would say, "Never again will you do rubbish like this. It is not worth it, not even for a million dollars." He followed this with the movie version of *Equus* for Sidney Lumet and was nominated for an Oscar for the seventh time. He didn't get it, but his fee was half a million and he got the part ahead of Marlon Brando.

At the end of 1976 he returned to Pontrhydyfen to show off Susan while he was narrating twenty-six episodes of *Vivat Rex* for BBC radio at a fee of £4,000 for two days' work. And he was back again in England the following summer to make *The Medusa Touch* for half a million at Pinewood. He was not drinking and seemed shaken by the death of his old friend Sir Stanley Baker. He quoted Dylan and wrote 'Lament for a Welshman' in *The Observer*.

Life with Susan was afternoon tea 'and no spare crumpet', said Dai Hopkins-the-Bread in the Miners Arms. 'Missed him you did by a couple of hours. He didn't hang about. Not the old Rich. He was polite and drank tonic water. Nice girl that Suzy.'

Nice? Polite? He always was.

Even when I last met him, we woke blank and eyeless at an empty table. Next morning we both received letters of apology from one another. He was now fifty-one and it had been a long, long time. I remembered walking down the high table at Oxford with the students banging their glasses on the boards and Richard standing in welcome with open arms. I remembered the 'only other genius from Oxford' that

Professor Coghill had taught, W.H. Auden, as Dai-
the-Bread showed a photograph of Richard and Susan
sitting together without excitement:

It's no use raising a shout
No, Honey, you can cut that right out.
I don't want any more hugs;
Make me some fresh tea, fetch me some rugs.
Here am I, here are you:
But what does it mean? What are we going to do?
It wasn't always like this?
Perhaps it wasn't, but it is.
Put the car away; when life fails,
What's the good of going to Wales?

Life with Suzy failed. Instead of putting away the
car, he threw out the fresh tea and drove down to the
local bar in the Swiss village of Gstaad. He made
another Where Eagles Dare with Richard Harris and
Roger Moore in The Wild Geese, Absolution for Elliot
Kastner and Breakthrough with Robert Mitchum and
Rod Steiger.

By the time he ended up in a neck brace after
surgery he was back on the sauce and many noticed it
as he was quietly tuned out of the commentary he was
doing during the Royal Wedding of Prince Charles
and Lady Di.

One night, a clear summer night in August 1981, he
was driving back from the village pub and became so
confused with the gears (he was driving an automatic)
that he managed to put his car into reverse and
collided with four other cars. He went through the
windscreen and the drivers of all four cars were
injured. A friend drove him home and Suzy had him
hospitalized to save him from police inquiry. The

following year, whilst sharing his bed with a woman journalist, a tape recorder and a bottle or two, he accused Suzy of sending him to 'the loony bin' and not a hospital. But his account of imprisonment in an asylum completely vindicated Suzy and showed that not only were his marbles seriously disturbed by the accident but that he was indeed a suitable case for treatment. He told the naked woman journalist that he was locked up behind bars for nine days and added: 'One day I was on the phone when a tall blonde woman with very tight trousers came over to me and said "Follow me". I thought it was Suzy and I followed her. She drew me down on a bed and we made love. Then I realized it wasn't Suzy at all but another patient — a nymphomaniac. They couldn't get her off me. Finally, when I was released from the loony bin I had to go to court and they sentenced me to a week in jail. That's when Suzy told me she wanted a separation.'

At the time of the brief encounter with the woman journalist he was making *Wagner* and complaining of being old and in pain. 'I can take my coat off, but I can't put it on again. I suffer epilepsy both *petit* and *grand mal*. I'm practically blind in one eye and my hands shake now with the exertion of lifting even as small a thing as a glass of vodka.'

As if to prove his crabbed age, he added: 'I have to hold the glass with two hands because the lifting muscles across the back of the neck and shoulders have been removed.'

After all this malarkey I wasn't too surprised to read that the woman journalist and the 'enfeebled' Burton went on a drinking marathon with the East German film star Eckhardt Schall, and that Burton drank him under the table and ended up wrestling in the gutter and proclaiming to the good burghers of Venice that he, Richard Burton, was the greatest actor in the world.

He was certainly fit enough to attend Elizabeth's fiftieth birthday party and prove, as he did to the woman journalist, that he was still 'a passionately cruel lover' in the wee small hours of the morning.

Indeed he seemed strong enough to wheel Elizabeth through the scenes of *The Little Foxes* when a couple of weeks later she appeared on stage at the Victoria Palace in a wheelchair after spraining her ankle.

Her very appearance in the theatre — she had never been on a professional stage in her life — seemed to prove what Burton had always maintained: that acting is a purgatory of boredom — a second-hand perch for the parrots of first-class minds. As Jack Tinker said of Elizabeth's performance (and he saw her when she wasn't in a wheelchair):

'Her first appearance in a cottage loaf wig and matching figure (had she by some mischance put on her bustle back to front?) was less than prepossessing. Not a woman in the place could have missed that the beaded burgundy dress was woefully unflattering to a lady of her generous girth and lack of height and the lacquered seasick wig only served to emphasise her generous helping of chin. Of course none of this tittle tattle would have mattered a jot had Miss Taylor been in the business of bringing new life to Lillian Hellman's complex heroine Regina ... But sadly this is way beyond the range of any stage technique she has acquired in her long and glorious career in films.'

Back in Venice Burton was playing Wagner as an old man of seventy. When he was called upon to lift the actress Gemma Craven he said: 'Gemma is tiny but I couldn't move her. My strength has gone.'

But his strength soon returned when he heard on the World Service about the Falkland Crisis. The stoop disappeared. He was marching about with a radio clamped to his ear. He was a trained pilot. One never knows. Joan Plowright, who was in the production, said: 'He told us he was a reservist and might be called up.' The wingless aircraftsman was romancing.

He was throwing off Wagner's old coat. Maybe he wouldn't require any help in putting on King Lear's heroic cloak.

At fifty-seven, age cannot wither, nor custom stale his infinite variety.

All his ladies, married or leading, have always said he is a better actor off stage than on. What they mean is he is always entertaining with a cheerful indifference to the fame and acclaim that other men seek with boring scholarship and grim determination.

Index

185

STAR BOOKS BESTSELLERS

FICTION

WAR BRIDES	*Lois Battle*	£2.50 ☐
AGAINST ALL GODS	*Ashley Carter*	£1.95 ☐
THE STUD	*Jackie Collins*	£1.75 ☐
SLINKY JANE	*Catherine Cookson*	£1.35 ☐
THE OFFICERS' WIVES	*Thomas Fleming*	£2.75 ☐
THE CARDINAL SINS	*Andrew M. Greeley*	£1.95 ☐
WHISPERS	*Dean R. Koontz*	£1.95 ☐
LOVE BITES	*Molly Parkin*	£1.60 ☐
GHOSTS OF AFRICA	*William Stevenson*	£1.95 ☐

NON-FICTION

BLIND AMBITION	*John Dean*	£1.50 ☐
DEATH TRIALS	*Elwyn Jones*	£1.25 ☐
A WOMAN SPEAKS	*Anais Nin*	£1.60 ☐
I CAN HELP YOUR GAME	*Lee Trevino*	£1.60 ☐
TODAY'S THE DAY	*Jeremy Beadle*	£2.95 ☐

BIOGRAPHY

IT'S A FUNNY GAME	*Brian Johnston*	£1.95 ☐
WOODY ALLEN	*Gerald McKnight*	£1.75 ☐
PRINCESS GRACE	*Gwen Robyns*	£1.75 ☐
STEVE OVETT	*Simon Turnbull*	£1.80 ☐
EDDIE: MY LIFE, MY LOVES	*Eddie Fisher*	£2.50 ☐

STAR Books are obtainable from many booksellers and newsagents. If you have any difficulty tick the titles you want and fill in the form below.

Name_____

Address_____

_____

Send to: Star Books Cash Sales, P.O. Box 11, Falmouth, Cornwall. TR10 9EN.

Please send a cheque or postal order to the value of the cover price plus: UK: 45p for the first book, 20p for the second book and 14p for each additional book ordered to the maximum charge of £1.63.

BFPO and EIRE: 45p for the first book, 20p for the second book, 14p per copy for the next 7 books, thereafter 8p per book.

OVERSEAS: 75p for the first book and 21p per copy for each additional book.

While every effort is made to keep prices low, it is sometimes necessary to increase prices at short notice. Star Books reserve the right to show new retail prices on covers which may differ from those advertised in the text or elsewhere.